CHICAGO PUBLIC LIBRARY
SOCIAL SCIENCES AND HISTORY
400 S. STATE ST.   60605

BS
192.6
.Y34
1996

Chicago Public Library

Yahweh--the patriarch : ancient ima

D0060747

Yahweh
the Patriarch

Ancient Images of God and Feminist Theology

Erhard S. Gerstenberger

Translated by
Frederick J. Gaiser

FORTRESS PRESS
MINNEAPOLIS

For Rita
esposa e companheira

YAHWEH—THE PATRIARCH
Ancient Images of God and Feminist Theology

First published by Fortress Press, 1996
English translation copyright © 1996 Augsburg Fortress

Translated from *Jahwe—ein patriarchaler Gott? Traditionelles Gottesbild und feministische Theologie*, published 1988 by W. Kohlhammer GmbH, Stuttgart.

All rights reserved. Except for brief quotations in critical articles or reviews, no part of this book may be reproduced in any manner without prior written permission from the publisher. Write to: Permissions, Augsburg Fortress, 426 S. Fifth St., Box 1209, Minneapolis, MN 55440.

Where not otherwise indicated Scripture quotations are from the New Revised Standard Version Bible, copyright © 1989 by the Division of Christian Education of the National Council of the Churches of Christ in the United States of America. Used with permission.

Cover design: Cheryl Watson

Library of Congress Cataloging-in-Publication Data

Yahweh—the patriarch : ancient images of God and feminist theology /
Erhard S. Gerstenberger ; translated by Frederick J. Gaiser.
   p.   cm.
   ISBN 0-8006-2843-8 (alk. paper)
   1. Masculinity of God—Biblical teaching.   2. Patriarchy—Biblical teaching.   3. God—Biblical teaching.   4. Bible. O.T.—Theology. 5. Bible. O.T.—Feminist criticism.   6. Bible and feminism.
I. Gerstenberger, Erhard.
BS1192.6.Y34   1996
231'.1—dc20
                                96-18044
                                CIP

The paper used in this publication meets the minimum requirements of American National Standard for Information Sciences—Permanence of Paper for Printed Library Materials, ANSI Z329.48-1984. ⊗

Manufactured in the U.S.A.   AF1-2843
00   99   98   97   96   1   2   3   4   5   6   7   8   9   10

Ro125 75 38 99

CHICAGO PUBLIC LIBRARY
SOCIAL SCIENCES AND HISTORY
400 S. STATE ST.

Contents

CHICAGO PUBLIC LIBRARY
SOCIAL SCIENCES AND HISTORY
400 S. STATE ST.   60605

Preface

The profound changes occurring now in our way of life necessarily affect church and theology as well. Are feminist inquiries into our traditional understanding of God just another part of the contemporary sociological revolution? Or has the ancient battle of the sexes now reached its climax—waged at last on something approaching equal terms? Whatever the answer, the church and its theology must ask itself troubling questions about the male dominance practiced on earth and visualized in heaven. This debate can only be conducted with relentless honesty and with full respect for everyone involved—those now living as well as our ancestors in the faith stretching back into biblical times. By the very nature of the case, even the most fundamental doctrines cannot escape critical inquiry, since even they are time-conditioned and time-bound. This pertains even to the confession of the one and only God; and it most certainly pertains to all human characteristics with which God is described, either consciously or unconsciously.

This book is a small contribution to a very extended dialogue. It arises from lectures, seminars, and many conversations with women and men. I am well aware of how much scholarly argumentation remains to be supplied. Nevertheless, I hope that what I say and write is not without value. Perhaps it can help in avoiding blind alleys and in developing new structures for church and society, structures that will harbor women and men on equal terms.

Introduction

The Question

"Daddy," said the four-year-old daughter of the pastor, "Does God have a penis, too?" For a moment, the pastor was speechless, but then he responded, "Of course not. After all, God is not a human being!" "But then why do we call him Father?" the child persisted. And her father could do nothing but point to the figurative nature of theological discourse. We ascribe to God characteristics and behaviors similar to those with which we are familiar. Fundamentally, God is "totally other." But from our limited perspective God acts like a "good father."

The child's question lays bare the greatest difficulty in all theological discourse. The deity, of course, is unknowable and unnameable. The nature of God evades human comprehension and surpasses our powers of imagination. Whatever good we think God represents, God's fullness and purity cannot be adequately portrayed in this finite and imperfect world. The great wonders of the ancient and the modern world—the goals of so many human dreams and pilgrimages—are just as incomprehensible from a distance. Only seeing them face-to-face can make an appropriate impression. Similarly, only a physical encounter with the deity could provide us a proper view of who God is. As human beings, we can come to know God, at best, only "in part," says the apostle Paul. Only face to face will our knowledge of God be complete (1 Cor 13:12). The Judeo-Christian traditions, as well as many other religions and philosophies, recognize the final incomprehensibility of God. With this in mind, theologians have often wondered whether it ought not be forbidden to speak of God. Anything that human beings say about God must of necessity be false. So should not people, including Christians, simply refrain from naming God or from attributing to God certain characteristic features? Aren't reverential silence and mute adoration the only possible stance before the unnameable deity?

Nevertheless, the people who founded the biblical traditions and grew up within them regularly threw caution to the winds and dared to speak of God. To the Jews, God's proper name, Yahweh, has been sacrosanct and unpronounceable since the third century B.C.E.; yet even they have replaced it with other terms like "Lord," "Shekinah" ("dwelling" or "presence"), or "Most High." They have not been able to avoid giving verbal expression to their experience of God. Again and again, the faith of those who stand in this tradition comes up against something awesome and overpowering, making itself known in the midst of everyday life. In both normal and extraordinary ways, history and nature portray events that directly signal the transcendence of the deity. Just as the sun remains recognizable behind clouds and fog, everyday life provides here and there a glimpse of the divine. Therefore, according to Judeo-Christian theology, we must speak of God, despite the imperfection of our language and of our imaginations.

Putting aside whether or not this argument is found convincing today, it remains clear that when human beings speak of God—at least as measured by biblically based notions of the nature and essence of the deity—they are attempting the impossible. Or, to put it another way, all talk of God introduces limited and incomplete (and therefore misleading) conceptions into our understanding of God. Human beings speak of God and, in doing so, always, consciously or unconsciously, presuppose their own circumstances and possibilities. Human beings speak of God according to their own human images. This pertains also to the perception that God is male. It is not that Jews and Christians have taken special pains to call God "he"; the masculine designation apparently developed "naturally" and without great to-do. God was seen as male because in ancient Israelite society—including the worshiping congregation—public and dominant functions were exercised only by men. Religion and the priesthood were reserved for men, and the ruling male elite quite naturally envisioned God in its own image, without question and without doubt. One is tempted to say that theology always works that way. It cannot be otherwise. Wherever people make statements about God, their own situation gets mixed up with the divine image. Age, gender, occupation, social status, every one of the theologian's life experiences colors his or her portrayal of God, even when God's transcendence, otherworldliness, and unconditionality are continually affirmed.

To a large degree, the history and consequences of the masculine portrayal of God remain to be studied, as do the isolated attempts by women and men within the Judeo-Christian tradition to overcome sexist portrayals and to draw into theology the experiences of women, children, and those who are socially powerless. At any rate, art galleries, works of literature, and biblical interpretations through the centuries demonstrate that the male view of God, as a reflection of society's patriarchal realities, is deeply embedded in the consciousness of Jews, Christians, and Muslims. To be sure, there have also been tolerant, comprehensive, and women-affirming religious expressions within the western patriarchal structures (among the Quakers, for example, or in the work of a few recognized female theologians). But overall the consequences of the masculine understanding of God have been disastrous. All too often, theologians, without reflection, have projected their experience of the polarity of the sexes into their image of God. So the woman was often turned into God's antagonist and thus the seducer, the heretic, the inferior human being. In fact, theologians occasionally even debated whether women (along with slaves, unbelievers, and degenerates) were complete human beings created in the image of God (see I. Raming).

Today's perspective—the contemporary social and ecclesiastical situation—necessarily gives rise to innumerable questions. Can God really be imaged only in male form? What happened to the female portrayals of the deity that produced the goddess figures of Israel's environment? How is it possible that within the biblical tradition the problem of the deity's gender went virtually unrecognized and unexamined for centuries? Why is it just now that people have begun open criticism of the male image of God?

The Christian notion of God has come under attack from many sides—a sign of the general revolutionary situation in which, for a variety of reasons, humanity now finds itself. The developing countries have seen the rise of an independent theology, one that—for European Christians surprisingly and painfully—has exposed the close connections between economic-political attempts at hegemony and the white European-American theological monopoly. Ecological and peace movements have discovered that both the relentless exploitation of nature and thoughts of military supremacy are, at their core, supported and motivated by religious notions, for example, the idea that an exclusive God has given superiority to the one group that has a claim on the deity. Racial minorities have charged that seeing God as white has been responsible for discrimination against and exploitation of entire population groups. And male and female feminist thinkers never tire of denouncing the close amalgamation of the still dominant patriarchal systems with the theological superstructure of a single, male, almighty Father-God. We need to consider all these questions as they have been put to traditional theology if we are to deal with the problem of the sexist alienation of God.

The feminist critique of God is relatively young, having arisen clearly and broadly only in our own time. Just thirty years ago there were virtually no questions of this kind. Where they did arise, as among fringe groups like the gnostic "sects" or the medieval Beguine convents, they simply went unheard by the church. Whether we read Karl Barth or Paul Tillich, Dietrich Bonhoeffer, or Edmund Schlink, or any other theologian from the 1930s to the 1960s, God is a being described unquestioningly with the male grammatical gender, one who cannot be thought about in female terms. Like the biblical authors before them, traditional theologians never particularly stressed this fact. The classification of God as a male being was simply assumed, as it had been for centuries. Theologians practiced it again and again, even while asserting God's transsexuality at the same time. Some would argue that this is only a minor issue, claiming that, after all, it is merely accidental that one grammatical gender predominates and, since this usage represents the whole, female human beings are included as well; but their number is diminishing rapidly. The unreflected maleness of God, which is somehow supposed to surpass all sexuality, is no accident; it is symptomatic of the religious structures that have defined the Judeo-Christian tradition from the beginning.

So how did God's "gender" ever become a problem? Without doubt, it was the women's movement that first seriously and comprehensively questioned the masculine imaging of God. The origin of the women's movement does not require detailed examination here. Suffice it to say that the French Revolution, American independence, and the beginnings of industrialization in the late eighteenth century signaled a revolution in all of life. New modes of thought and production touched the existence of the family and resulted in a transformation of all social structures and human relationships. Centuries-old understandings of roles, social orders, and behavioral norms began to change. Since the mid-nineteenth century, women have organized to fight for equal rights and a voice in economics and politics. In Germany, for example, Luise Otto Peters and Helene Lange were successive leaders of the Allgemeiner Deutscher Frauenverein (General German Women's Organization), which meant to provide women participation in the destiny of the nation. In 1879, August Bebel published a manifesto with the title *Die Frau und der Sozialismus* (*Woman and Socialism*), in which he wrote, "Our goal then is, not only to achieve equality of men and women under the present social order, which constitutes the sole aim of the bourgeois woman's movement, but to go far beyond this, and to remove all barriers that make one human being dependent upon another, which includes the dependence of one sex upon the other. *This* solution of the woman question is identical with the solution of the social question." And a little later: "*For there can be no liberation of humankind without social independence and equality of the sexes*" (A. Bebel, 7).

So, for more than a hundred years, there has been both a middle-class and a socialist women's movement; a corresponding stream in the church has either been lacking altogether or, at best, a tiny rivulet (see E. Moltmann-Wendel, *Frauenbefreiung*, 48ff.). Church and theology still remain firmly in the hands of men, even though here and there a few women have found a hearing and tried to influence theological terminology. The primary impulse for the emancipation of women has come from various political and social movements outside the church. Only after more than a hundred years' delay have they spread to and affected the church, thereby newly throwing open the God question in our own time. Up to the 1960s one heard virtually nothing in church and theology about the equality of women and the patriarchal imaging of God. Even in the United States, there was little conversation about this in ecclesiastical circles. The civil rights struggle for blacks claimed all the available energy. But then—following upon the Second Vatican Council, the struggle for racial integration, and the increasing sense of an economic North-South dependence, with its incumbent exploitation—women, including female theologians, began to stir. In *The Feminine Mystique* (1963), Betty Friedan demythologized the male idealization of the feminine as an instrument of domination, another kind of contempt. The "new image of the woman [in the 1950s] as housewife-mother has been largely created by writers and editors who are men." Men had returned from the war in which they "had been dreaming about home and a cozy domestic life" (Friedan, 54). Now they pushed women back into the kitchen and nursery, raved about femininity and sex, and rigorously took public affairs into their own hands.

Then, in 1968, Mary Daly took aim at the church's discrimination against women in her book *The Church and the Second Sex*. She followed up in her second book, *Beyond God the Father* (1973), with a radical renunciation of the Judeo-Christian tradition. This volume was a milestone in the development of feminist theology. It totally rejects the biblical portrayal of a Father-God as the offspring of patriarchal arrogance and lust for power. Daly relentlessly uncovered the religious roots of the male struggle for predominance. She wants nothing more to do with the Christian-Jewish religion because in her opinion the biblical faith in God is, at its very core, an exclusively male faith to which women have no access. Thus, she says, one should no longer attempt to reform the biblical images. They are not remediable; there is no chance of humanizing them and giving women a stake in this male religion. The biblical Father-God must be "castrated" and replaced by a yet-to-be-discovered dynamic and integrating understanding of God. Just as Malcolm X, in the name of black America, had previously renounced the irredeemable white God of oppression, now Mary Daly renounced the fundamentally sexist God of the Bible and of the whole Judeo-Christian tradition.

Here we see the issue most acutely. Even in their titles, official church utterances of the postwar era—for example, the World Council of Churches' study "Sexism in the 1970s" (Geneva, 1975) or the investigation commissioned by the council of the German Protestant Church on "Die Frau in Familie, Kirche und Gesellschaft" (The Woman in Family, Church, and Society; Gütersloh, 1979)—evade the real theological question about the portrayal of God. Discussions by contemporary male systematic theologians (still?) seem not to take the feminist critique of God with great seriousness. Perhaps it has not even been noticed. Is this because male theologians still operate according to the old principle that women should be silent in the churches (1 Cor 14:34)? Or does the church still regard women as incapable of contributing to its theological teachings? It is not outside the realm of possibility that the female majorities within the churches might take seriously the rejection of a male God, and then the unity—indeed, the very existence—of the church would be at stake. So, the burning question is this: Does our biblical tradition necessarily present and presuppose an exclusively male picture of God, growing out of a hopelessly patriarchal society? Or, prior to and alongside the Israelite Yahweh and the Greek Kyrios, were there mother deities that have somehow been fused together with the patriarchal images of God? Today, as a consequence of women's liberation and the search for valid theological expressions exercised by women more and more self-consciously, do we need to recover from our tradition the mother deity that existed either before or alongside the Christian Father-God?

The theological concerns expressed in these feminist inquiries are fully justified. Whether battle cries like "Back to the Goddess!" or "Make way for female spirituality!" provide a genuine and contemporary answer remains to be seen. In my view, the issue is whether female experience and female personhood will be able to find their proper place in portrayals of God, theological discourse, and the life of the church. Today's emancipation of women must have its effect on the shaping of the symbols and central concepts of theology. Just as both female and male citizens rightly demand to be taken into account by their national constitutions, so the gathered experiences of all the faithful must find expression in the formulation of a church's teachings. How God is imaged is a response of the community, of the people of God, to the address of an unconditioned, unnameable, absolute deity. But the response reflects the concrete conditions in the life of those responding. And since women can no longer be excluded from social and ecclesiastical responsibility, the theological response must also encompass female experience. How we image God is always changing and developing. The issue for today is: What picture of God will be true, honest, appropriate, life-giving, and community-building?

Whence Our Image of God?

How will or how can we arrive at a response to these theological inquiries and critiques? To understand the current theological issues we need to ask about their origins. To correct false developments we need to establish a case history and form a diagnosis. Specialists agree that the switches determining the track to our present theological perspective were decisively set in the first millennium B.C.E. For our own culture, the most important influence came from the biblical people of Israel. So, above all, we need to question the biblical witnesses, as these are available to us in the Hebrew canon. The decisive issue is the understanding of God presented there and the conditions that made it possible for that understanding to continue into the present day.

So the Bible is the first and most important source for our research into the causes of the present situation. We will choose a few texts from the Hebrew canon that are significant for our topic and examine them. How did the perspectives on sexuality and the relation between the sexes of that day find their way into theological assertions? When did the concentration on a one-sided and exclusively masculine portrayal of God begin? It is quite possible that the ancient Israelite authors were simply unaware of the issue as we have posed it here. Moreover, texts are something like tracks in the snow: they don't reveal everything. In fact, texts veil or keep secret unpleasant facts and developments. Certainly, statements about the gender of God have always been among the most delicate of theological topics; they touch the most basic self-interests of gender and occupational groups. Therefore, we cannot merely declare the canonical texts normative and ignore as heretical any contradictory testimonies denounced by the biblical authors. The Bible cannot be interpreted so easily and uniformly. Indeed, the canonical texts themselves are not free of tensions. They must always be seen over against the concrete background of the time in which they were written or handed down; they must be interpreted in conversation with the dominant views, interests, and social structures of their own period.

Extrabiblical testimonies can be very helpful to the critical reading of biblical texts. Of primary importance will be inscriptions and artifacts discovered through archaeological excavations in and around Israel. These documents have survived intact through the centuries and, unlike the biblical testimonies, have not usually been reinterpreted and adapted by succeeding generations. Therefore, they permit us a direct insight into the religious situation of the time of their origin. Secondarily, a comparative and panoramic view of the religious world of the peoples surrounding Israel will be extraordinarily important for Old Testament scholars. Is it not strange and, for our topic, perhaps decisive that all of Israel's neighboring cultures found sexual differentiation among their deities entirely natural and theologically necessary, while in Israel alone (at least in later times), Yahweh, the solitary and exclusive God of heaven, ruled over a people that was seen either as given to him in marriage or bound to him by covenant? The biblical witnesses know full well about the clash between Israel's faith in God and their neighbors' faith in the gods. We, too, can make use of our knowledge of ancient oriental cultures to help in our interpretations, especially where it is a question of understanding Yahweh's claim to solitary rule.

However, given our topic, it will be insufficient merely to channel all our energy into the analysis of ancient texts and archaeological discoveries. It will be equally important, and perhaps even more so, to remain in conversation with one another, to consider and discuss the inquiries of our own day, especially those of women affected by patriarchal images of God and ecclesiastical practice. This will require us regularly to reexamine our own positions. This is the only route to genuine learning. An objectifying study of ancient sources without reference to our own situation would lead only to a collection of data fit for a museum. Our interpretations and reflections must critically draw in today's realities as well. Consequently, our question goes far beyond merely paying attention to theological tracts about an appropriate conception of God for our time. The whole contemporary relation between men and women is at issue, the broad effects of patriarchal ideas of God on social and ecclesiastical life. It is a question of the intimate relationship between unjust social orders and false understandings of God, of the liberation of all people who have suffered under patriarchal claims to dominion.

The portrayal of God that we seek together certainly has something to do with the perspective of the individual seekers. It is therefore right and salutary that the author of such a study define his own particular point of departure.

As a biblical exegete and theologian, I make use of historical-critical, form-critical, and social-critical methods. I will not define these in great detail here. Suffice it to say that historical distancing and analysis of past documents belongs to the essence of our culture and cannot easily be replaced by various attempts to achieve an immediate encounter with a text or a biblical event. We have grown accustomed to view things objectively, a perspective that has certain advantages as long as one remains conscious of the fact that a fair measure of subjectivity continues in all our striving for objectivity. Even as an engaged scholar, I remain bound by my origins and entanglements. The two other methodological areas, form criticism and social criticism, merge for me. Form criticism implies that every ancient text exhibits a certain language pattern that can and does betray the life situation of the text. However, in every case this *Sitz im Leben* is a socially conditioned point of contact, and without such a social contact-point no text can be understood or interpreted. Therefore, I regularly try to go through the form and genre of a text to discover its social setting; from there, using the social sciences, I attempt to comprehend each textual statement in its social context.

As a citizen and a human being, I live in the northern hemisphere of this earth, with its enormous economic and political privileges. I did not grow up in favelas or slums but in an industrial society that, despite having lost a war, won participation in a sophisticated system of global domination. European prosperity is produced or financed by the majority of the world's population that is underpaid, hungry, and illiterate. The consequences of this for the prevalent notions of God and probably even for my own idea of God are not hard to picture; they are easily discernible in the ecclesiastical and social reality of our time. The dominating, judging, enemy-destroying God, who occasionally shows up looking like Superman or Rambo, is quite popular in our day and our society.

As a man whose patriarchal orientation came primarily from my own mother, I grew up with the traditional hierarchy of the sexes. We are prisoners of our own inherited and carefully nourished roles and will probably never be able to shake them off. Nevertheless, experiences in other countries, in my own marriage, and in my pastoral work have provided me certain self-critical insights. And even though I am not by nature in a position to bring women's experience into the theological discussion, I can at least try to expose the competitive male display behavior hiding behind many theological declarations. Moreover, it seems to me that a critical and open male contribution to the present theological discussion of feminist challenges to our imaging of God is dangerously underrepresented. Theological truth can only be approached by the open conversation of everyone involved.

1 | Yahweh, the Father

Israel's history began with the migration to Canaan sometime in the thirteenth to twelfth century B.C.E. Six hundred years later its political history came to an end. We will start with that endpoint, which also represents a theological line of demarcation, and attempt to trace the development of Israel's faith in God backward in history. In doing so, we will distinguish the following main periods in Israelite history: the exilic and postexilic period (587–200 B.C.E.), the time of the monarchy (1000–587 B.C.E.), and the tribal era (1300–1000 B.C.E.).

Almost all experts agree that Old Testament theology reached its high point and entered its formative phase only after the loss of national independence, with the subjection of the people of Yahweh to the great powers of Babylon and Persia. Several things came together to create the phenomenon called "theocracy" or divine rule, Israel's specifically "ecclesiastical" form of organization. These factors included reflection on the past; gathering the religious traditions (including putting them in written form); a focus on Jerusalem, the spiritual capital; the worship life of those who remained at home and those who were dispersed; and common festivals, customs, and practices. The religious community of the people of Yahweh survived the catastrophe and, in those critical decades following 587 B.C.E., created for itself a common foundation of faith, a common picture of God, and several modes of religious communication. These enabled the nation's survival even under foreign rule and despite the dispersal of the people throughout the then known world.

Researchers are less certain about whether the exclusive worship of the one male God, Yahweh, was also a product of the sixth

1

century. Many want to see the roots of Yahweh's claim to exclusivity in the earliest beginnings of Israel's history, or even earlier, in the time of the patriarchs. For them, God's revelation to Moses on Mt. Sinai (Exodus 3 and 6) would be the latest possible firm beginning date. The religious history of Israel would then run its course, from about 1300 B.C.E. onward, as presented in the several biblical historical outlines. According to these texts (for example, Deut 1–3; 2 Kgs 17; Ps 106), Israel repeatedly abandoned Yahweh, the one and only true God—in the desert, in the period of the judges, and during the monarchy—only to discover once more at the very end of its autonomous history (that is, at the time of Josiah) the notion of "one God, one temple, one lawbook." However, especially according to the Deuteronomic history of the sixth century B.C.E., their rediscovery came hopelessly late (2 Kgs 22–23); Yahweh's long-predicted judgment had become inevitable. Israel's task was to preserve the faith in one God through the catastrophe and reconsolidate it after the collapse.

This picture of Israel's history seems credible to me only if one recognizes it as a tendentious and systematic exercise, projected backward on the past. Of course, in this sense, all historical pictures are backward projections or ways to control the past. Even so, we must not give up the attempt to comprehend historical epochs on their own terms and to reconstruct the course of history as it actually unfolded step by step. When we do that with the history of Israel, several sources (e.g., the oldest strands in the historical books and the prophetic writings) lead us to the conclusion that, prior to the exile, Israel had gone through various stages of polytheism and henotheism (the preferential worship of one deity) before it finally arrived at the patriarchal monotheism of the exilic period (Israel's normative century). To be sure, we need to say this with appropriate caution. We know, first, that even such a supposedly objective view of history projects contemporary notions and systems on the past, and, second, that the various stages that marked the way to Israel's monotheistic faith of the sixth century did not follow one another in a deliberate manner; instead, in the unfathomable course of history, they developed in a highly contradictory and discordant fashion—after, alongside, and within one another. The discussion of this new view of Israel's religious history began only a few years ago. In German, three volumes, published by Roman Catholic Old Testament scholars Othmar Keel, Bernhard Lang, and Ernst Haag, are by far the most accessible results of this discussion (in English, see R. Albertz, *History*). No matter how much one might disagree with the details presented by these scholars, one central thesis seems to me to be correct: the exclusive worship of the one and only God Yahweh emerged in that form only in the century of the exile as a response to Israel's special problems and experiences. Patriarchal monotheism is a particular creation of that particular century and is not comparable to previous forms of the preferential worship of a national deity. Of course, the theologians of the exile made use of elements of the earlier tradition (how could they not have done so?), but out of these available elements arose for the first time a radical faith in one God that had previously not existed in the same form.

If this is true, we can see the exile as a decisive turning point in the faith of our spiritual ancestors. We can isolate this late phase of Israelite theology, the end of one epoch and the beginning of another, and pose our questions to the documents coming to us from that period. Why did Yahweh become the dominant patriarchal God at that time? Were other deities, especially female ones, suppressed or forced underground?

From the many biblical materials of that period, we will examine first a passage that seems to offer a clear answer. Then we will ask this text about its context and its relation to the rest of the Old Testament.

Isa 63:7–64:11 is a communal liturgy of lamentation. It arises from the exilic community's intercessory worship and, following the destruction of the temple and the triumph of the enemies, seeks to motivate Yahweh to turn away from his wrath, to return to Israel, and to give help and mercy to his people. The hymnic, lamenting, and intercessory elements of this liturgy reach their peak in the three-fold address, "You are our father." The emphasis on Yahweh's fatherhood always appears in the context of an impassioned petition for divine care. Consider, for example, Isaiah 63:15–16:

Look down from heaven and see, from your holy and glorious habitation. Where are your zeal and your might? The yearning of your heart

and your compassion? They are withheld from me. [But] you are our
father, though Abraham does not know us and Israel does not acknowledge us; you, O LORD, are our father; our Redeemer from of old
is your name.

Again, at the end of the liturgy, a new series of petitions is introduced with the intensified expression, "Yet, O LORD, you are our
Father" (Isa 64:8). The address or cry of the congregation, "Our
father," seems to have programmatic significance in this prayer of
lamentation. Yahweh is held fast to his responsibilities as relative.
Human ancestors, like Abraham and Jacob, can no longer help,
but Yahweh, the divine ancestor, does have power and can demonstrate it in acts of liberation within Israel's history; thus, it is
from him that freedom and blessing can now be expected or even
demanded. As father, as the nearest and most important relative,
he has an obligation to redeem his sons who have fallen prisoner
to their own wrongdoing. Moral and legal ties require the father,
even the divine father, to intervene.

What does this text's use of the title "Father" have to say to the
topic at hand? Yahweh is made subject to Israel because of his
fatherhood, something that happens rather rarely in the Old Testament (see Hos 11:1–3; Isa 1:2; 45:9–11; Jer 3:19; 31:9). The
praying community apparently wanted to activate Yahweh's superior power. But why not through the use of the normal image of
the warrior king? The title "King" is still used freely for Yahweh
by the communities of Israel after the collapse of 587 B.C.E., as,
for example, in the royal psalms (Pss 47; 93; 96–99) and in Isa
41:21; 43:15; 44:6. However, in Isaiah 56–66, the third part of the
book of Isaiah (Third Isaiah), Yahweh is never addressed with this
familiar title. The word "king" is reserved for foreign rulers (Isa
60:10–11; 62:2); Yahweh is addressed only with epithets like the
"Holy One," "Mighty One," and "Lord." But the issue at stake,
the demonstration of Yahweh's ruling power for the sake of his
people Israel, is very much in evidence in Third Isaiah. Yahweh
is displeased that there is no justice for his people and promises
to use power to help them (Isa 59:16–20). In Isa 63:1–6, Yahweh
the warrior is fully in action: "I trod them [the Edomites] in my
anger and trampled them in my wrath; their [blood] spattered on

my garments, and stained all my robes." The fact that this warlike God is addressed in our text with the familiar name "Father" certainly has something to do with the structure of the praying community, which no longer knows a king and for which the head of the family is the most important and most commonplace authority.

The father concept, as figuratively applied to Yahweh in Third Isaiah, includes ideas of biological motherhood as well. The final chapter of Isaiah contains this sentence, now often quoted: "As a mother comforts her child, so I will comfort you" (Isa 66:13). From our perspective, it is unnatural and contrary to biology to speak of God both as the one who impregnates and as the one who gives birth, but two other Old Testament texts (Num 11:12 and Hos 11:3) seem to require the same conclusion. This reflects a religious idea broadly held in the ancient Near East. Whatever the deity's gender, its powers surpass human understanding and make it able to appropriate the functions of both human genders. For example, the Egyptian gods Amon and Aton are occasionally addressed in prayer as both the father and the mother of humanity. Similar ideas can be found in Mesopotamian literature. Yet, despite this ambivalent use of titles, the deity should not be thought of as a hermaphrodite. Nor should we conclude from the religious language of the Old Testament or from ancient Near Eastern literature that older notions in which male and female deities functioned in ways contrary to their gender somehow meant biological hermaphroditism. What is going on here is merely an inclusive way of speaking that applies only to the deities in their "total otherness," not to the realm of human experience.

If calling God Father in Third Isaiah arises from existing social conditions and recognized cultic hierarchies, and, furthermore, if seeing Yahweh as father primarily emphasizes God's protecting function, then it is clear that our text describes neither the actual sexual nature of God nor the place of women in the community. Yahweh is addressed as Father because in that world the father was the normative and responsible figure. If the Israelite men and women of the exilic generation wanted to use something other than the common designations of God, Savior, or Redeemer to refer to Yahweh, the only possible comparison from the realm of the social institutions was father. There is no evidence from the book of Third Isaiah that this nomenclature needed to be established polemically against other divine epithets. There was only one God for the prayers of the lament liturgy, and he is logically compared to the male head of the family. There is no sense of competition with a goddess in our text. Nor does the polemic against the idols in Isa 65:3–5 suggest the cult of a female deity. The accusations presented there betray rituals involving nature, the dead, and the sacrifice of pigs, but the people addressed and accused are obviously men. For the orthodox believers represented by the unknown author of Third Isaiah, Yahweh was incontrovertibly a single, male deity. The apostates had turned to foreign cults that are not clearly definable.

It is noteworthy that the congregation regarded itself as the son or child of the divine father. Usually, it is presented instead as the wife or beloved of the male God (cf. Hos 2:16–22; Jer 3:6–10; Ezekiel 16); this is especially true in the immediate context of our prayer of lamentation (cf. Isa 62:4–5). Both pictures arise from family life and are taken into theological language from that sphere. Both signal the congregation's dependence upon and security in Yahweh. Both call forth the mutual responsibilities of family members as these were established in the laws and customs of that time. The figurative references to Yahweh as Father and to Israel as son emphasize more strongly that God has given life to his people. They also emphasize the fact that the congregation stands permanently under God's direction and guidance. On the other hand, they open the possibility of childish rebellion. Like members of an ordinary family in that day, Israel, too, could evade its duties as a son, go its own way, and rebel against its father (Isa 1:2; Deut 32:6, 18; Jer 3:19–20). But in the critical postexilic period, the term father is used with a different theological significance: a devastated Israel now employed the father-son relationship to try to preserve its tie to the old God. The covenantal relationship to Yahweh, which is described by many Old Testament authors, is based on a historical decision made by Yahweh and the people at a particular time. The father-son relationship on the other hand is, one that might be called "natural" or given; it cannot be easily revoked by either party. The concern of the lament liturgy in Isaiah 63–64 is to hold fast to the sonship of the community of Israel. It employs "Father" (just as it uses images of God as husband and bridegroom) to appeal not to Yahweh's choice but to his obligations as caregiver.

Later, in a small collection of homilies and disputations, the problem of Yahweh's designation as father turns up again. "A son honors his father, and servants their master. If then I am a father, where is the honor due me? And if I am a master, where is the respect due me? says the LORD of hosts to you, O priests, who despise my name" (Mal 1:6). The whole composition, handed down under the name or title Malachi (which means "my messenger"), reflects the congregation's deep insecurities about proper cultic practice and conduct of life. The anonymous speaker or author continually argues against rebellious questions and all attempts to justify divergent behavior. The father title for Yahweh is also found in this context. It seems to have common acceptance in the community; but the problem is that the behavior (at least of the priests) doesn't correspond to the assertion that God is our father. Children owe their father subordination and respect. But these are denied to Yahweh. Contempt for his authority has become widespread. The narrator of these theological arguments sees Yahweh reacting more and more sharply (see Mal 1:10–11) and assuming higher and higher authority. In these sermonic fragments, God moves out of the familiar father relationship and assumes once again the role of absolute ruler. "I am a great King"—like the Persian emperors of that time—"and my name is reverenced among the nations" (Mal 1:14).

It is therefore all the more remarkable that, following a bitter conflict with the priests, the father designation is again applied to Yahweh in a (penitent?) response of the congregation. "Have we not all one father? Has not one God created us?" (Mal 2:10). The theme is quite different from the one in Mal 1:6. Here the descent from a common father is meant to lead the children, that is, the congregation of believers in Yahweh, to act in solidarity. The speakers complain that this is not the case. The self-evident application of the father title to Yahweh emphasizes once again the use of the name in popular theology and piety. Further, the collective statement provides yet a third meaning for the father concept in

Israel. Alongside the protective and nurturing functions of the father, on the one hand, and his undisputed authority, on the other,
now the paternal power of procreation quite clearly becomes the
theological point of comparison (see Jer 2:27; Deut 32:18).

Two areas of concern remain to be discussed: first, how did
calling Yahweh father arise in Israel; and second, what was the
understanding of patriarchy in that time?

The father designation is used for the God of Israel emphatically but somewhat problematically in the postexilic collection of
texts in Third Isaiah and Malachi. That usage leads to the suppo-
sition that the postexilic period was the origin of the theological
address "our Father." (The use of the father image for Yahweh
in Hosea and Jeremiah would need separate investigation.) That
would certainly be understandable: During the separated or
united monarchies, Israel had a form of government and society
in which royal titles were appropriate for Yahweh. But after the
collapse of 587 B.C.E., old and perhaps long forgotten divine epithets turned up again, clearly deriving from familial and tribal
relationships; among these was the name "father." Many personal
names in the Bible and in Israel's ancient Near Eastern environment show that individuals within the family could also be
thought of as son (or child) of a deity, a creature owing allegiance
and standing under the deity's protection. Eliab ("God is father"),
Abiel ("father is El"), Abijah ("father is Yahweh"), Joab ("Yahweh
is father")—these are only a few examples of names showing this
child-father relationship. They were gender neutral and could
be given to either newborn boys or girls. To be sure, almost all
people known to us with divine names of this kind are men, since
even the early familial religion already followed the male line.
The use of such names implied more than biological origins; it
ascribed to the individual member of the group a very personal
child-parent relationship with the family's protecting deity. We
will surely not go wrong if we assume the entire family or tribe
analogously saw itself in childlike dependence upon the paternal
(and/or maternal) deity. Thus, the names for God that express an
individual relationship (my God, my King, my Redeemer) play an
important role in the familial cultic practice of the ancient orient

(see H. Vorländer); in the Old Testament, too, one occasionally finds the title "my Father" (Ps 89:22 [27]; see Job 17:14). In other words, from the beginnings of Israel's religious history the deity was seen in relational terms, especially within the familial cult. Because of the dominant patriarchal structures of the day, designating God as father took precedence. Naming Yahweh "Father" was taken up, again advisedly, in the postexilic community, possibly to establish a deliberate distance from national metaphors such as King, LORD of Hosts, and so on. In this way, later Old Testament theology oriented itself to the small, familial cultic situation of earlier times, which to some degree had been overrun and suppressed by the centralized monarchical theology of the national era.

Thus, in the Old Testament, the designation of Yahweh as father takes on totally different dimensions from those we might suspect on the basis of the contemporary discussion of patriarchy. At that time, "father" and "paternal" did not have the same abusive, emotional, or comic connotations they have now. The reason for this was the different social structure. For most people of the ancient world the family was the only real place of security (this was the ideal for all people: women, children, and men of all ages); it was the place where life and work took place. The individual could develop only within the family. It offered the financial, spiritual, and religious structure for a full and meaningful life. And everywhere the family was patriarchally constituted—though there may have been local and ethnic nuances. Externally, the father or family chief represented the group. Internally, there was a precisely defined hierarchy with its respective assignments. As a rule, the primary wives had their own rather broad areas of domestic responsibility. Here and there women could also take on public tasks (see W. Römer). In the Old Testament, at least, the requirement to be veiled and the prohibition against appearing in public were unknown. There was no social order besides this male-governed, yet thoroughly bipolar, family structure. Indeed, given the way of life and division of labor of that time, an alternative would have been completely unthinkable (see S. de Beauvoir, E. Badinter). The common life and common work within the family group (which was, to a degree unimaginable for us, an autonomous economic unit) was strictly ruled in every way by customs and norms. Each family member assumed a position determined by age, gender, and social status. This ranking obligated each person to serve the whole group, but also preserved rights of personal development and involvement in decisions. The family (today we would say "extended family," since different generations, a variety of relatives, and servants all lived under one roof) was the normal social structure. The Old Testament knows nothing of a permanent solitary life, and other forms of communal life were possible only in extreme cases and at the fringes of normal society (see 1 Sam 22:2; 2 Kgs 6:1–2). From today's perspective, the patriarchal structure of the family group appears tedious for men, discriminatory against women, and unjust. We live in an industrialized society that long ago did away with the old family structures, including also its image of the father (see A. Mitscherlich). Working from this historical experience, we might well condemn the ancient patriarchal structure wholesale. The fact is, however, that no such fundamental critique was ever uttered in biblical antiquity, and the patriarchal extended family was a stable social microstructure growing out of the contemporary living conditions and means of production. The man's power to use women (and children and slaves), rightly found offensive today, was probably balanced to some degree by the dominant position of the woman in the household (see 1 Samuel 25; 2 Kings 4).

Let us return to our theological questions. How shall we evaluate the Old Testament's patriarchal view of God? Is it still appropriate to call God "Father," a name that presupposes ancient familial structures? Provisionally, we can say the following:

1. Like all names for God in all languages and religions, the father designation in the Old Testament is a figurative and indirect mode of theological speech. It reflects the peculiar patriarchal conditions of life in the Near East, which are comparable to those of the late twentieth century in only a limited way. The father name for Yahweh is used unreflectively, at least as far as its sexual connotations are concerned. The texts never attempt to polemicize against female realities. Rather, the fatherhood of God includes all kinds of parental care (see Ps 103:13). No discrimina-

tion against or exclusion of women is intended by this manner of speaking. The same cannot be said quite so easily with regard to the image of Yahweh as Israel's lover and husband. More will have to be said about that later.

2. The postexilic community's return to the use of the old father title, common in the earlier familial cults, originally had a positive sense. It indicated not only an alert theological consciousness, but also a renunciation of national delusions and a theological relativizing of larger social organization in general (in Israel, the now-defunct monarchy). Faith in God and openness to the absolute occur primarily and authentically in the small circle of an intimate group. Religion based on some kind of mass organization is very quickly, and to a far greater degree, susceptible to the corrupting influence of the exercise of power. As contemporary Christians with centuries of triumphalistic church history behind us, we must recognize that biblical faith is, in its essence, a faith that functions within immediate, face-to-face human relationships. Most of all, it offers help and liberation to those who are oppressed. What the "our Father" of the postexilic texts wants to say is that God dwells among the least and the most despised. The surprisingly intensive use of the name Father by Jesus and the early Christian community has precisely the same sense (see also J. Jeremias).

3. It follows that the image of father is scarcely usable in theology today. Among confirmation classes and certainly among reflective women, the image awakens false associations with antiquated claims of authority. In reality, fatherhood no longer functions as a model in our atomized society. "Father goes to work, is never at home, does not understand children, and dies early of stress"—these are the central elements of fatherhood for today's school children. Mother is also not highly esteemed—for different, though certainly related, reasons. So, is there any need at all now for names for God that come from the realm of small human groups? I think the answer is yes. If we examine our human relationships, our way of life, and our desires, we may come to the following conclusion: If we were to name God today in analogy to our relationships with other people, we would have to use expressions like "sister" or "brother" or "friend." Metaphors

drawn from these relationships would perhaps best express the good news of God's solidarity with the human race. On the other hand, images from hierarchical family structures (especially in their nineteenth-century form) are no longer usable, because, at least ideally, this order has been overcome by more democratic notions.

2 | Ishtar, the Queen of Heaven

In Israel, faith in the one and only God Yahweh coalesced in the sixth century B.C.E. It was a matter of course that this one God had male characteristics. We have seen that the concept of father did not, in itself, include sexual discrimination against women. In other texts, too, the male point of view arose "naturally," reflecting the dominant social conditions. "And seated above the likeness of a throne was something that seemed like a human form," says Ezekiel in his throne chariot vision (Ezek 1:26). "Something that seemed like an Adam" is the Hebrew expression; and we can be certain that every biblical passage that speaks of Adam refers primarily to a male human being rather than a female. The few other Old Testament descriptions of visions refer without hesitation to Yahweh as LORD. "I saw the LORD sitting on a throne, high and lofty" (Isa 6:1). "I saw the LORD sitting on his throne" (1 Kgs 22:19). When the Israelites spoke of God in analogy to human beings, they did not see him as gender-neutral, but always and exclusively as male, a view that has remained virtually untouched through the centuries up to the present time.

This fact is surprising. Were female deities entirely unknown in Israel, despite their broad distribution throughout the surrounding cultures and religions? Were no questions or challenges leveled at the developing male image of God during that formative sixth century? Were Israelite women from the beginning limited exclusively to the male God Yahweh?

A remarkable and unique text in Jeremiah 44 reports an open confrontation between the prophet and the adherents of the cult of a "queen of heaven." Though the reference is veiled, other texts (1 Kgs 11:5 and 2 Kgs 23:13) make clear that Jeremiah speaks of a single female deity and not the "host of heaven" or a "swarm of created heavenly beings." This goddess is probably identical with the astral deity Inanna or Ishtar, worshiped in the Orient since ancient times (see D. Wolkstein). We will look first at the passage in question and then ask about its background and surroundings.

In Jer 44:1 we find one of those stereotypical titles that now divide the book of Jeremiah into separate sermonic units: "The word that came to Jeremiah." This formula comes from a group of theologians of the exilic period, called "Deuteronomists" because they based their theology on the book of Deuteronomy. The formula may already reflect a worship practice of reading and commenting on the words of the prophet. As in some other passages, Jer 44:1 includes, after the formula, a precise description of the situation in which this particular revelation is given. Jeremiah has found asylum in Egypt with a group of Judean refugees. The refugees are distributed among the cities of Migdol, Tahpanhes, Memphis, and in the land of Pathros (that is, in lower, middle, and upper Egypt). In other words, the narrator's scope is quite broad. The sense of the urgent message delivered by the prophet to all the exiles in Egypt is this: The disaster has come upon you, Jerusalem has been destroyed, and you know why! The cause is your apostasy to other gods. And now what? warns Jeremiah, according to this passage. Do you want to throw away all chances of survival by further idolatry? This admonition and this accusation, found in vv. 2–14, are fully in the style of Deuteronomic preaching.

And then comes the astonishing reaction of those addressed— men "who were aware that their wives had been making offering to other gods" (v. 15), and the women themselves, who did nothing "without our husbands' being involved" (v. 19). Both groups respond in unison. Nowhere else in the Old Testament do the opponents of Yahweh present their own point of view so eloquently:

> "Instead, we will do everything that we have vowed, make offerings to the queen of heaven and pour out libations to her, just as we and our ancestors, our kings and our officials, used to do in the towns of Judah and in the streets of Jerusalem. We used to have plenty of food, and

prospered, and saw no misfortune. But from the time we stopped making offerings to the queen of heaven and pouring out libations to her,
we have lacked everything and have perished by the sword and by famine." And the women said, "Indeed we will go on making offerings to
the queen of heaven and pouring our libations to her; do you think
that we made cakes for her, marked with her image, and poured out
libations to her without our husbands' being involved?" (vv. 17–19)

However one classifies Jer 44:15–19 historically and literarily
(there is a parallel in Jer 7:16–20), the passage certainly reflects
opinions and problems of the Israel of the exilic period, if not
those of the Egyptian diaspora. The following comments make
use of the work of Urs Winter, who has carefully worked through
this text (Winter, 561–576). The writers and readers or hearers
of this text were obviously familiar with a cult of the queen of
heaven that was in competition with Yahwistic faith. In other
words, the people who formed the book of Jeremiah were in a
totally different situation than those who shaped Third Isaiah.
What was the nature of this goddess religion, chiefly conducted
by women? Apparently, the worship of the queen of heaven was
practiced in Jerusalem, among other places, and involved the entire family. Children gathered wood, fathers kindled the fire, and
women baked sacrificial cakes (Jer 7:18). The women's contribution to this prohibited form of worship seems to be regarded as
the most important. Women also take the lead in Jeremiah 44:19.
The central cultic act is the preparation and presentation of a simple breadlike cake, probably in the shape of the revered goddess
or bearing her insignia. That is the sense of the expression in v.
19: "marked with her image." Forms for baking such cakes both
in female shapes and as star-shaped symbols have been found in
Mesopotamia and Syria. In the palace at Mari on the Euphrates
River alone, forty seven such forms were discovered. A Phoeni-
cian clay model portrays a holy baking ritual along with the usual
seals. Four women work at an oven preparing the sacrificial cakes
(Winter, 568ff; Winter also reports the rules for the ritual presentation of the cakes). Briefly stated, in a widespread household cult,
bread and ash cakes—part of the basic nourishment of that
time—were offered to the gods along with libations; women had
primary responsibility for all of this. For our interests, that means

the critique of the national Yahwistic faith in Jeremiah 44 comes from the sphere of home and family; it comes from the women who were responsible for this cult (see chapter 5).

But we would like even greater precision. To whom were these sacrifices made by the Israelite women (with the agreement and help of their husbands and children)? Winter thinks it might naturally be Ishtar, the Assyrian goddess of heaven. On the other hand, the Mesopotamian cult of Ishtar was significantly influenced by the original mother- and earth-goddess, worshiped since prehistoric times. This goddess cannot be identified by name (see Winter, 192–199), but she was known already in Greek antiquity as the Syrian goddess. She is always pictured naked, seems to be called upon predominantly as an intercessor and helper of private people, and came only secondarily to be counted among the primary deities, perhaps as the partner of the gods Adad, Baal, or Assur. It is important for us to note that, as Winters's extensive work demonstrates, archaeological excavations find traces of this goddess in the region and period of Israel's history (contrary to J. H. Tigay). Many figures of the naked goddess have been found in Israelite cities from the period of the monarchy, primarily in excavated private homes. It is significant, though, that the transmitters of Jeremiah 44 have shifted the scene of the goddess cult to Egypt. They may have had in mind the Isis cult, though the name "queen of heaven" has not been found applied to this Egyptian deity, and all the cultic forms described in Jeremiah 44 actually point toward the Syrian/Mesopotamian region. Localizing the activities related to the queen of heaven in Egypt may simply be a literary device meant to push such an "abomination" as far away as possible, placing it in this impure foreign land. The reference to earlier cultic practices in Jerusalem (v. 9) and the location of the "cult of abomination" in Jerusalem by the parallel text (Jer 7:17) clearly demonstrate that the original locale of the goddess cult was Canaan and Israel.

Before turning to the details of this goddess worship in Israel, we can already conclude that among certain circles or in certain situations at the time of the exile, people were (still or again) faced with the alternative: Yahweh or the queen of heaven. Or, to put it more cautiously, in these instances, the alternative to Yahweh was a single female deity who, like Yahweh, appeared without a marriage partner. Over against her, the champions of Yahweh argue for the exclusive recognition of their God. The sexual polarity seems to play only a subordinate role in this struggle. At any rate, the queen of heaven is not condemned because she is female. Nor is Yahweh preferred for his male gender, but only because he is the guarantor of Israel's survival.

How does Jeremiah 44 depict this form of idolatry? We have already called attention to the unusual breadth of the argument allowed to the apostate women and their husbands. Alongside their own decisive rejection of Yahweh and their similarly decisive attachment to the local goddess (vv. 16–17a) stands their defense of the unorthodox cultic practice through reference to the "ancestors, kings, and officials" in Jerusalem. (This stereotypical list occurs in other places in the book of Jeremiah as well.) Then comes the theological counterattack: As long as we worshiped the goddess, things went well for us and our families. The goddess fulfilled her protective function. It was the Yahweh cult that brought misery, defeat, and deportation upon the people (vv. 17b–18). Might this resurgence of Yahwism refer to a suppression (perhaps a violent one) of goddess worship in Israel? The words suggest otherwise. The misery began with "the time we stopped making offerings." This sounds more like the rejection of the goddess was their own doing. The text also says the women carried out the cult of the queen of heaven with the knowledge of their husbands (v. 19). Thus, female initiative and patriarchal oversight or co-responsibility are uniquely lifted up here. The brief parallel passage in Jer 7:19 reports only that the family cult involved children, fathers, and mothers, in that order.

How should we evaluate the description in Jeremiah 44? The narrator appears to present not an accurate picture of conditions in Jerusalem before its destruction, but instead describes a religious problem of his own time, as he understands it, using his own language and basic theological perspective. Representatives of the Yahweh faith and those of the goddess cult are in dispute. There is no "official" religious authority that can issue laws and ordinances to bring the conflict to an end.

Jeremiah's response, as described by the narrator, also makes this clear. Jeremiah contradicts in detail the defensive and accusatory speech of the women and asserts exactly the opposite. One assertion stands over against another. Now it is the worship of the queen of heaven that is said to have brought defeat and deportation upon the people (vv. 21–23). The broad generalizations and theological abstraction of the prophet's speech are in the preaching style of the Deuteronomist. It presents nothing new by way of content, but merely gives a brief explanation for the present desolate condition of the congregation. Then, however, it expands into a speech of admonition and warning for the exilic period. Divine judgment is pronounced upon the Jewish colony in Egypt: Yahweh's name will no longer be pronounced on the Nile (v. 26). The refugees there "shall perish by the sword and by famine" (v. 27). And those few who escape death will return to Judah disconnected and bankrupt (v. 28). The entire unit (vv. 24–29) comes together and concludes with the offer of a sign: Yahweh will punish the Judeans in Egypt in order to make clear that his words will be carried out. The following concrete historical announcement (v. 30) is probably a later addition: like the Judean King Zedekiah, Pharaoh Hophra will fall to the Babylonian conquerors. We know from both Egyptian sources and the Old Testament that Hophra was in fact defeated by Nebuchadnezzar, though his actual death came in the internal Egyptian battles of 569 B.C.E. (see Jer 37:5). Thus, the Israelite narrator seems to draw together various Egyptian losses to the Babylonians with no great interest in precise historical accuracy, using this review to form his prophecy against Hophra. If that is true, we must place Jer 44:30 in the period after 568 B.C.E. More interesting to us, however, are the admonitions the exilic narrator or preacher draws for his own time from these events (that have been placed in the time of Jeremiah). He obviously wants to say to the exilic community as clearly as possible: "You subjugated and dispersed Israelites can expect no help from the queen of heaven. Your chances lie with Yahweh alone, the traditional God of Israel." Does he have sexist motives for speaking this way? Is he promoting the male deity Yahweh at the expense of the female queen of heaven? I don't think so. The passage includes none of the vocabulary of marital infidelity. Moreover, women are never portrayed as tempting others to idolatry, as they are in other pertinent biblical passages (see Deut 13:6 [7]; 1 Kgs 11:4). In our texts, the men and children support the cultic activity of the women, as was apparently quite customary in domestic cults. It seems the narrator's point is simply to make clear which deity actually has the power to reestablish this defeated and humiliated people of Israel. Surprisingly, given this theological issue, the alternatives he envisions are either Yahweh or the queen of heaven. In other words, the experience of the one who shaped these two passages in Jeremiah shows that other gods or pairs of gods are de facto not among the options. Among the many possibilities within his polytheistic environment, the only candidates for the office of God in Israel are the two deities named here. Significantly, with this choice the Israelite narrator contrasts two deities of totally different levels of society—Yahweh, the God of the entire people; and the queen of heaven, here seen as a familial goddess. The congregation's task at that time was to build a new theology on the ruins of the old religion of the nation and the clans. It is difficult to determine whether memories of what may have once been an official cult of the queen of heaven in Jerusalem play a role here (see 2 Kgs 23:13).

From today's perspective, working from our own theological questions, the events described in Jeremiah 44 look different. We want the text to respond to our own contemporary problems—a legitimate desire, even though these problems were unknown to the narrators and preachers of that day. National and religious identity and the danger of apostasy to other gods do not play the same role for us that they did for the defeated and dispersed people of Israel. We know nothing of a tension between familial religion and communal religion, since familial religion, like the family itself, has become powerless. Instead, the burning questions for us are questions about women's spirituality and female portrayals of the deity. And, interestingly, the competing "other" deity in our two Jeremiah texts happens to be female. The women were decisively involved in the cultic worship of the goddess. So what would be more natural than to find here a lost female religiosity and a patriarchal onslaught against the matriarchal religion of women? And, in fact, many women read these Jeremiah texts as witnesses to a supposedly once dominant pre-Yahwistic goddess worship (see E. Sorge, 54ff.).

The broader background for this interpretation of the Jeremiah pericopes is the much-discussed matriarchal hypothesis of Johann Jakob Bachofen. In this view, a supposed early preeminence of women and goddesses was replaced in prehistorical times or at the beginning of documented history (that is, in the fourth and third millennia B.C.E.) by a male seizure of power. This change was thought to be brought about by the transition from a culture of food-gathering to one of settled farming in which the ownership of the means of production shifted to men (see E. Borneman). Alternatively, it is simply male evil per se that is responsible for this reversal of the order of the sexes and the resultant exploitation of women (see H. Göttner-Abendroth). In my opinion, such views of history belong in the same category as stories about the fall into sin. The indisputable element of truth in the fall narratives lies in their polarizing of current chronic problems of society and faith. However, as soon as they set the conflict between good and evil within chronological history, things become quite problematic. The same is true with an alleged original healthy and peaceable matriarchy that was supposedly replaced by a warlike, brutal, exploitive, and misanthropic patriarchy. Neither archaeology nor sociology, neither anthropology nor psychology (see M. Mitscherlich), provide sufficient evidence for a historical epoch of matriarchy. The hypothesis becomes completely insupportable with the realization that its basic concern, gaining individual equal rights for women, is a modern question, arising only out of the Enlightenment and modern industrial society (see U. Wesel; or, with different accents, E. Badinter; I. Illich). Preindustrial movements toward emancipation arose and developed more sporadically and did not fundamentally challenge family structures and the distribution of roles (see chapter 8).

The arguments for or against an original matriarchy would, of course, have to be examined much more carefully than we can do here. Above all, we would have to consider exegetical evidence, especially from the Judeo-Christian account, par excellence, of the fall. The story of the fall in Genesis 3 is interpreted in some feminist literature (but not only there) as though it spoke of an original paradise that was lost forever because of human rebellion, that is, a solitary act of disobedience. Of course, in the feminist interpretation the break between the old world and the new comes through Yahweh, who, in his patriarchal hunger for power, dethrones the goddess Eve (see H. Göttner-Abendroth; E. Sorge; R. von Ranke-Graves). But, in fact, the biblical story of the fall speaks about paradise and the world's perversity not historically but mythically. What the mythical story describes as two periods, following one after the other, is nothing other than the ebb and flow of life known from human experience. Sometimes paradise and hell are experienced one after the other, sometimes concurrently. They do not describe epochs of world history. In Genesis 3 the polarity between the sexes plays an essential role for the biblical narrator. The woman lures the man into disobeying the deity and is therefore more seriously punished than the equally sinful Adam. As a result the social hierarchy is set in patriarchal terms. The woman must subordinate herself to the man (Gen 3:16). None of this, however, is historical memory of matriarchal conditions; it is a way to legitimate prevailing patriarchal claims to leadership that have been operative as far back as human beings can remember (S. de Beauvoir). Perhaps the story existed only to soothe the male conscience; or it may present a teasing challenge to women: Don't you see now why you are only second rate? Many tribal societies have stories of this kind in which (usually) men, in pretended indignation, tell of women's impertinence and need for recognition, using this to justify male predominance (see N. Pereira). The patriarchal order is never seriously questioned in the ancient world or in the biblical writings. Even the book of Ruth, written totally from the woman's perspective, serves the interests of patriarchal family structures completely and exclusively. No, Genesis 3 is not about an early degradation of women, but rather describes the prevailing conditions in the clan and family units. These have always been patriarchally ordered in the Orient, as they still are. Even less does the fall story refer to an older myth about combat among the gods. That Yahweh defeated Eve, the primal mother, and even appropriated her name is pure speculation. Neither the text of the fall story nor analogous myths of

the ancient Orient nor material available to us from historical lin-
guistics provides evidence for any such hypothesis (contra R. von
Ranke-Graves).

However, the loss of the matriarchal hypothesis does not end
the justified theological concerns and demands of women. Rosemary Radford Ruether correctly formulates the present view of
things:

> If all language for God/ess is analogy, if taking a particular human
> image literally is idolatry, then male language for the divine must lose
> its privileged place. If God/ess is not the creator and validator of the
> existing hierarchical social order, but rather the one who liberates us
> from it, who opens up a new community of equals, then language about
> God/ess drawn from kingship and hierarchical power must lose its
> privileged place. Images of God/ess must include female roles and expe-
> rience. Images of God/ess must be drawn from the activities of peasants
> and working people, people at the bottom of society. Most of all, images
> of God/ess must be transformative, pointing us back to our authentic
> potential and forward to new redeemed possibilities. God/ess-
> language cannot validate roles of men or women in stereotypic ways
> that justify male dominance and female subordination. Adding an im-
> age of God/ess as loving, nurturing mother, mediating the power of
> the strong, sovereign father, is insufficient. (R. Ruether, 68–69)

The feminist challenge to traditional theology is fully and
completely justified by the habits of life and thought, the values,
and the human relationships operative in the modern world. Our
society has become individualized. Every human being stands before God directly. The human person is now a religious subject as
an individual, not only as a member of a family or group. At least
in theory, women have achieved equality with men in vocation,
law, and public life. Thus, they rightly demand that women's experience also find its place in theology and in the imaging of God.

The misunderstandings leading to the construction of a matriarchal history begin with a naive reading of biblical and mythological texts. We cannot simply presuppose that the women and
men of antiquity (not to mention our own parents and grandpar-
ents) were conscious of the contemporary issue. If ancient texts
are to answer modern questions, they can do so only by the diffi-

cult means of comparing and contrasting the situations in ancient and modern times. From a certain perspective, Jeremiah 44 is in fact a revolutionary text. In relative openness, it wonders whether the old national religion is still up to the task, whether it can provide the basis for making sense of the catastrophe, suffering, and doubt of the exile. Almost impartially, it asks whether the worship of the goddess from older times might not again be appropriate in this crisis. Obviously, the narrator decides for Yahweh, LORD of hosts, the God of the fallen kingdom. Isaiah 63–64 decided for the father, the familial patron deity. Comparing the two texts shows with full clarity the flexibility and variety in the (patriarchal) Israelite portrayal of God. The texts also bear witness to the philanthropy, even the love, of the God being addressed. Among the alternatives, although it is rejected, one "even" finds a female deity. For the most part, contemporary theologians (Karl Rahner is an exception) shy away from seeing the "goddess" as a conceivable alternative. But Jeremiah 44 can give us the courage to seek diligently for a way to speak of God that includes women's experience and women's reality. The female element belongs to the substance of theology. It was already included in the patriarchal religion in a form appropriate to the social setting (see P. Trible, *God and the Rhetoric of Sexuality*). In view of the new equality of the sexes, the participation by women in theology and church—long neglected and suppressed in the Judeo-Christian tradition—must now be accorded its rightful place. At the same time, at least in passing, we must also note, of course, that the biblical stories provide us not only with analogies to our own issues and questions, they also stand over against us critically. The individualization of our faith, our privileged standard of living, and, not least, the lust for power on the part of both men and women are all unmasked in confrontation with the biblical texts (see chapters 9 and 10).

3 | *Yahweh and His Asherah*

It is not easy to sketch an accurate picture of the theology of the royal period (1000–587 B.C.E.), primarily because the historical sources deriving from that epoch—which ran from the tenth century (Abimelech, Saul, David; see Judges 9; 1 Samuel 9–1 Kings 1) to its catastrophic end at the beginning of the sixth century (see 1 Kings 2–2 Kings 25)—were thoroughly revised in the century of the exile and totally reinterpreted from the theological perspective of that later period. So we have to try to reconstruct the operative ideas of the royal period from revised texts; this requires a critical analysis of the relevant writings and reports. In addition, we will have to appeal to the relatively few written documents brought to light by archaeology. They have the advantage of being precisely datable and having undergone no reinterpretation. Other archaeological discoveries, such as the figurines of female deities and the architectonic remains of cities and temples, can also help us reconstruct the monarchy's understanding of God. Naturally, contemporaneous extra-Israelite parallels will also be exceedingly important, though we can investigate these only in passing.

The picture gained from the Old Testament itself—above all from the books of Samuel and Kings, but also from the classical prophets and a few older psalms—is not uniform. If we take away those characteristics of Yahweh recognized and known only in the exile—uniqueness and exclusivity, universality and heavenly transcendence—the only thing remaining for the theology of the royal period is Yahweh as the national God of Israel. He was very closely tied to the royal houses of Judah and Israel (the Northern Kingdom). The movement toward a state religion was consciously introduced by David when he brought the old, nearly forgotten ark of the covenant to Jerusalem and annexed the royal sanctuary (2 Samuel 6). Admittedly, his ecstatic dance in front of the ark on that occasion was sharply criticized by his favorite wife, Michal. Does her critique imply an attack on the state religion because of its male orientation? Hardly. Its real concern is the self-degradation of the royal majesty, which the later writers found unbearable (2 Sam 6:20–22). The cultic nudity for which David is reproached, is, of course, more appropriate to a fertility religion than to some kind of transsexual patriarchal religion. In any case, David introduces Yahweh as the state deity, and the divine declaration guaranteeing the continuance of the Davidic dynasty comes as a response to David's efforts at making Yahweh the national God (2 Samuel 7; cf. Psalm 89). By building the temple, David's son Solomon consolidated the national religion (1 Kgs 6:8)—if, in fact, the temple was built by Solomon and had not already been built by David. However, after the division of the monarchy in 926 B.C.E., each of the resultant states went its own way in religious matters. In the Northern Kingdom, sanctuaries were built in Bethel and Dan, which the southerners regarded as heretical (1 Kgs 12:26–13:5). We learn virtually nothing about the actual religion of Yahweh in the North or the understanding of God found there. Even though the Elijah stories, the words of the prophets Amos and Hosea, and parts of the Pentateuch arose partially or completely in the North, these, like all Old Testament writings, were later subject to a Judean revision—which at many points is easily recognizable (see Hos 1:6–7; Amos 2:4–5; 9:11–12).

So what we know about the religion of the royal period is this: Yahweh was the national God. He was worshiped in the royal temple in Jerusalem, which was the national temple first of the united Davidic monarchy, and then (as we learn primarily from sources passed down in the South) of the smaller Southern Kingdom and its Davidic dynasty, still ruled from Jerusalem. At least that is the official picture of the religion of that day. Old Testament scholarship has begun to distinguish between the official religion and the popular religion of the royal period, especially as the latter was practiced outside of Jerusalem in the rural areas and villages (see R. Albertz, *Persönliche Frömmigkeit*; H. Vorländer; B. Lang; M. Rose). Let us look first at the religion of the country-side. What did those people think about God? How advanced was the patriarchal shape of religion outside Jerusalem? A full investigation would have to contrast the prevailing notions in the capital city with the religion of the rural areas, all of which would take us too far afield. Instead, we will examine two particular texts to try to gain an overview of the popular religion of the royal period.

In the countryside, the ancient sanctuaries at the high places, mostly of Canaanitic origin, existed more or less uncontested alongside the national temple. What do we know about these local sanctuaries? What deities were worshiped there? Most of these sanctuaries were open-air shrines without full temples. The origin of just such a holy place is described in detail in Genesis 28:10–19. A traveler is spending the night in the wilderness. In a dream he sees divine beings climbing and descending a ladder. Upon awaking, he becomes aware of the significance of the spot where he had his dream:

> "Surely the LORD is in this place—and I did not know it!" And he was afraid, and said, "How awesome is this place! This is none other than the house of God, and this is the gate of heaven." So . . . he took the stone that he had put under his head and set it up for a pillar (*maṣṣebah*) and poured oil on the top of it. He called that place Bethel." (Gen 28:16–19)

This is a typical legend about the founding of a shrine, which has a certain general applicability. Every region has its shrine and probably a similar story about its origin. That it was Yahweh who was said to have appeared in Bethel is a later reinterpretation. Actually, as shown by the play on words in the name of the site, it was the god El who here revealed himself.

Traces of these high places (Hebrew *bamah* = back [of an animal or person], ridge; or, according to other authorities, hill of sacrifice or hill of the dead) can be found everywhere in the royal period. Even Solomon visited the principal high place at Gibeon (1 Kgs 3:4), despite the fact that it was his own father who had founded the sanctuary of Yahweh in Jerusalem. The justification given for this in 1 Kgs 3:2, that there was no proper temple at that time, is a pretense of the exilic period meant to protect Solomon from the accusation of crass idolatry. At Gibeon, the king receives an important revelation in a dream (1 Kgs 3:5–15).

During Samuel's travels through the villages and cities, he established a popular sacrificial festival at an unnamed shrine (*bamah*—1 Sam 9:12–14). As a young man, David was commanded by his brothers to attend a family sacrifice in Bethlehem (1 Sam 20:29). The same David, while he was still a guerrilla leader, assured himself of the support of the priests of the sanctuary at Nob (1 Sam 21:1–9[1–10]). The broad condemnations of the high places as well as the occasional references to reform in the works of the later Deuteronomist and of some prophets are sufficient proof that the judgment of modern history is correct: "Even after the building of the temple in Jerusalem . . . the *bamoth* continue to be regarded as legitimate cult places" (K. D. Schunck, 132).

The references and polemics allow quite a detailed picture of the furnishings at these nature sanctuaries. Certainly the most important element was the sacrificial altar. Almost every passage speaks of the sacrifices and incense offerings presented at the high places. Archaeology confirms this record. For example, a paved area with an open-air altar from the Bronze Age was found in Megiddo; reached by climbing a flight of stairs, it had a diameter of eight to ten meters. A rectangular platform unearthed in the city of Dan may be a similar high-place altar. More important for us are the repeatedly mentioned stone pillar (*maṣṣebah*) and wooden pole (*'asherah*) found, along with the altar, at the high places. These two cultic objects clearly indicate a sexual differentiation among the deities. The *maṣṣebah*, a simple, vertically placed stone (as described in Genesis 28) is, at the least, a symbol of the presence or preferred location of a male deity, if not directly of the phallus or the divine power of procreation. In either case, the stone is a holy symbol with patriarchal significance. In addition to the *maṣṣebah* there was a wooden pole, a symbol of a sacred tree. Its very name, *'asherah*, is the Hebraized form of the name Ashratum, Ashirta, or Athirat, a consort of the gods and mother deity, attested in the Ugaritic texts especially for Canaan and Syria. The *maṣṣebah* stone and the *'asherah* pole are often mentioned together in the Old Testament. This is especially true in the stereotypical Deuteronomistic condemnations of the worship of such stone pillars and sacred poles (Exod 34:13; Deut 7:5; 12:3; 16:21–22; 1 Kgs 14:23). Strangely, the Bible does not associate these objects with the god El and his Asherah, as in Canaanite religion, but with the divine pair Baal and Asherah (see Judg 3:7; 6:25–26; 2 Kgs 21:3; 23:4). Both deities are sharply opposed by the Deuteronomist (see 1 Kings 18, in which Elijah prevails over 450 prophets of Baal and 400 prophets of Asherah). Nevertheless, we can certainly assume that during the entire royal period the cult of the high places, existing near or within the villages, was tolerated alongside the official cult of Yahweh in Jerusalem; it may even have been seen as the self-evident form of local worship, a necessary addition to the national religion. In other words, at least in the popular religion outside the capital, there were sexually differentiated deities. In order to determine the role played by goddess worship during the time of the monarchy, we will examine two particular texts, pursuing further the phenomenon of the local Israelite cults.

Judg 6:25–32 tells how Gideon destroyed the Baal-Asherah cultic site that his clan, one that apparently had considerable political importance, had established at Ophrah in northern Israel; in its place he erected an altar to Yahweh. As much as we might like to see this report as a document about the introduction of Yahwism from the premonarchic era itself, this hope will not be satisfied.

Certain characteristic phrases (compare, for example, the "tearing down" of the altar and the "cutting down" of the sacred pole in Exod 34:13 and Deut 7:5) and favorite ideas (for example, the absolute contrast between Yahweh and the other gods) betray a later Deuteronomistic revision. Above all, the explanation of the name Jerubbaal at the end of the story (v. 32), toward which the entire episode flows, shows an anachronistic discrepancy. One would hardly expect Gideon, the contender for Yahweh, to be renamed for the defeated god. In fact, the interpretation of the name in this verse ("Let Baal contend against him") is just as improbable as the one in Gen 32:28 [29], in which Israel is said to mean "You have striven with God and with humans." If we were to proceed from the normal meaning of the name Jerubbaal ("Baal contends [for him]"), we would have to conclude that the bearer of the name stood in a positive relationship with Baal. Therefore, Gideon must actually have been a Baal worshiper who converted to Yahwism or one who worshiped Yahweh under the name Baal. In any event, the story of the destruction of the Baal-Asherah cultic site at Ophrah has been fundamentally rewritten and reinterpreted under the Yahwistic influence of a later time; thus, we can no longer be sure of its original contents. The only certainty is that cultic places for a pair of deities like Baal and Asherah existed in Israel before the introduction of an exclusive Yahwism. We must leave open the question of why, in the Old Testament, Baal does not consort with Anat-Ishtar as he does in the Ugaritic texts. But, significantly, we do learn that the worship of a god/goddess pair existed in Israel during the royal period, and that this was seriously challenged in the later revision of this text. The revisionist concern had nothing to do with sexual differentiation; Baal and Asherah were foreign gods that had to make way for the one God Yahweh.

There does, however, seem to be a sexist bias at the center of a second group of texts. Take, for example, 1 Kgs 11:1–8, a summary of Solomon's cultic practices. We do not even need to compare the stereotypical rebukes of other kings to determine that this passage, too, comes from the pen of those later theologians of the Deuteronomistic school who retrospectively condemn the entire royal period:

> King Solomon loved many foreign women along with the daughter of Pharaoh: Moabite, Ammonite, Edomite, Sidonian, and Hittite women, from the nations concerning which the LORD had said to the Israelites, "You shall not enter into marriage with them, neither shall they with you; for they will surely incline your heart to follow their gods"; Solomon clung to these in love. Among his wives were seven hundred princesses and three hundred concubines; and his wives turned away his heart. For when Solomon was old, his wives turned away his heart after other gods; and his heart was not true to the LORD his God, as was the heart of his father David. For Solomon followed Astarte the goddess of the Sidonians, and Milcom the abomination of the Ammonites. So Solomon did what was evil in the sight of the

LORD, and did not completely follow the LORD, as his father David had done. Then Solomon built a high place for Chemosh the abomination of Moab, and for Molech [n.b.: most likely a copying error for Milcom] the abomination of the Ammonites, on the mountain east of Jerusalem. He did the same for all his foreign wives, who offered incense and sacrificed to their gods.

This text, with its unevenness and repetitions, is certainly not a single unit. It displays at least three separate opinions regarding the question of the responsibility of Solomon's wives for his idolatry. In v. 7, perhaps the oldest element of the text, Solomon acts completely on his own, for no reason at all. Verse 8 assigns the guilt to the foreign wives. Finally, v. 4 blames the king's idolatry on the weakness of old age, which makes him yield to the influence of the wives (this certainly intends to offer some excuse for his actions).

What can we learn regarding our topic from this multilayered text? The second and last king of the unified monarchy almost certainly had a large harem. This was appropriate to his political position and immeasurable wealth, which are so conspicuously extolled in 1 Kings 10. Historically speaking, it is highly doubtful that the king's wives, of all people, were responsible for his diverse altar building; in common practice and in the view of the royal marriage song, Psalm 45, such wives had to subject themselves completely to their husbands. The admonition to the princess marrying into Israel is "Forget your people and your father's house" (Ps 45:10 [11]). International marriage contracts in the ancient Near East do not provide for the free exercise of religion by royal daughters given into foreign marriages. Thus, in ascribing all responsibility for idolatry to the king's wives, the text exhibits a later, perhaps priestly, prejudice, one that finds similar expression in the story of the fall (Genesis 3) and the narratives about Queen Jezebel (1 Kings 21) and Queen Athaliah (2 Kings 11).

In actuality, it is more likely that Solomon was motivated by internal political concerns, quite apart from the influence of his wives, when he built high places near his capital; these shrines for the Moabite God Chemosh and the Ammonite God Milcom were virtually within sight of Israel's national temple. We know some things, though not enough, about these two deities. Milcom, sometimes called Molech or Moloch in older translations, was usually related in Israelite tradition to human sacrifice, especially child sacrifice (see Lev 20:2–5; Zeph 1:5; Jer 49:1–3). We know about Chemosh from several Old Testament passages and, above all, from the inscription of the Moabite King Mesha. In this unique document, the national god of Moab (Israel's neighbor to the east) orders a war of conquest and retribution against Israel; the entire population of the area of Israel called Nebo is sacrificed to him. The god's name is recorded on the stone as Ashtar-Chemosh. It is not clear whether this is a double name, the name of two deities, or a god/goddess pair (cf. Pritchard, 320; however, in a later inscription from the third century B.C.E. the name of the female partner of the Moabite god is Sarra—see Beyerlin, 262).

Like 2 Kgs 23:13, our text accuses Solomon of idolatry not only to Milcom and Chemosh but also to Astarte (1 Kgs 11:5). This verse derives, of course, from the obviously judgmental late level of the text, whereas v. 7 apparently arises from a list of building projects honoring foreign deities that was still value free. Astarte, in v. 5, is termed "the goddess of the Sidonians." Even in this latest redaction she is not called an "abomination" as are Milcom and Chemosh. Astarte is the Greek form of the Canaanite name Ashtarat. Like Ishtar and Anat, this goddess is one of the astral or heavenly deities rather than a dispenser of fertility. She has warlike characteristics and in Ugaritic mythology is clearly differentiated from Athirat/Asherah—although that does not, of course, exclude the possibility that local cults may have connected or interchanged the two goddesses. In both 1 Kgs 11:5 and 2 Kgs 23:13, Old Testament tradition retains the singular form for Astarte/Ishtar; otherwise, the Old Testament references are plural (*ashtaroth*) and occur in summarizing texts describing idolatry or the reformation of idolatrous cults.

Thus, the passage 1 Kgs 11:1–8 reproaches King Solomon for his idolatrous relationship with three national deities of smaller neighboring states, all of them mentioned by name. Among them are two male deities and one female. The respective partners of these gods are unnamed, perhaps because their existence went without saying and because, as a rule, only one primary god or goddess represented a state's affairs. In the final redaction, Astarte, Chemosh, and Milcom are seen as examples of foreign gods in general (v. 4). Solomon's wives are said to be at fault for his apostasy to all three (v. 2). The particular cults of the Egyptian, Edomite, and Hittite wives (v. 1) are not mentioned. Accordingly, the historical issue behind this passage is the encouragement and toleration of Canaanite cults on Israelite soil outside Jerusalem. With the exclusive concentration on the cult of Yahweh after the catastrophe of 587 B.C.E., all foreign deities and all cultic places except the temple in Jerusalem are declared completely illegitimate. We have seen that one late level of Old Testament tradition ascribes to women a peculiar inclination to apostasy from Yahweh or to a return to native religions. This "susceptibility" to foreign cults, however, does not indicate a preference for goddesses on the part of the foreign women or a particular campaign directed against female deities on the part of the exilic theologians. As already stated, what it signifies is the resistance of the later period to *all* foreign gods.

The Old Testament texts reveal a varied and colorful religious life during the monarchic period. This picture is confirmed and amplified by the discoveries of biblical archaeologists.

To be sure, because of their comparatively sparse furnishings, open-air sanctuaries are often very hard to find or identify, though they are clearly mentioned in the Bible. Archaeologists can more easily identify temple complexes within a city, but there are fewer biblical references to these. Such temples are mostly of pre-Israelite Canaanite origin, and it is difficult to show in each instance whether the building continued to be used under Israelite rule. However, an actual Yahweh temple was found in one southern Judean city, Arad. Evidence shows that the small sacred building comes from the royal period and was already destroyed prior to the catastrophe of 587 B.C.E. The astonished archaeologists uncovered a court with an altar of burnt offerings and a broad temple area with a small incense altar and a centrally located cultic niche. In the niche, the temple's holy of holies, obviously stood a limestone stele, once painted red, which was meant to represent nothing other than the presence of the God Yahweh. The cultic stele is a typical *massebah*. One can only speculate whether the niche also contained a symbol of a female deity (see O. Keel, *Symbolism*, fig. 248).

Inscriptions that could inform us about the Yahweh cult of the monarchic period are extremely rare. As examples, consider three tomb inscriptions that, despite their brevity, are of great interest. They were found in Khirbet Beit Lei near Lachish: "Yahweh is the god of all the earth. The mountains of Judah belong to him, to the god of Jerusalem"; "The (mount of) Moriah thou hast favored, the dwelling place of Yah, Yahweh"; "Deliver, Yahweh" (J. Gibson, 58; K. Smelik, 166–167). The last sentence is a personal prayer like those occurring frequently in the Psalms. In the middle sentence the short and long forms of the name Yahweh occur together, and the holy mountain mentioned is known from Genesis 22. In the first sentence, Yahweh is both the universal God of the whole earth and the city God of Jerusalem. All three graffiti speak only of the one God Yahweh (the dating is uncertain; see K. Smelik, 165).

The situation is different in a few texts known through excavations only since 1975. They come from a small village named Kuntillet Ajrud in the Sinai area of southern Judah and from Khirbet el-Qom, west of Hebron. They speak not of Yahweh alone, but of "Yahweh and his Asherah," at least according to the most probable interpretation of these texts. For a popular discussion of these discoveries, see the articles in *Biblical Archaeology Review* by Z. Meshel and A. Lemaire (see also J. Day; U. Winter, 486–490; K. Smelik, 150–167; and F. Stolz [in O. Keel, *Monotheismus*, 167–173]). Since the texts are so remarkable, they are quoted here in full (as cited by R. Albertz, *History*, 1:86).

The two inscriptions from Kuntillet Ajrud were found on clay shards within the fortress. It is possible there was a school for scribes in that distant outpost, a pilgrimage site of the Judean kings. The pupils would have written their lessons on clay shards, a common practice in the ancient world. The clay shards or jars on which the inscriptions were written also include various drawings, among them two humanoid figures that most likely portray Yahweh and his consort. The texts, written in an early form of Hebrew, are difficult to decipher because the ink has faded and the word order cannot always be clearly determined. The first inscription reads:

> Amaryaw says: say to my lord, "Is it well with you? I bless you through Yahweh of Teman and through his Ashera, may he bless and protect

you and be with my lord. Whatever he asks of anyone may it find
favour . . . and may Yahweh give him his heart's desire!"

Apparently this is a fragment of a letter. Most important for us
is the personal blessing formula, which remains almost completely intact. The text first mentions two dispensers of blessing:
Yahweh and his Asherah. Then it repeats the blessing in the third
person masculine singular.

The second text, in its best preserved section, is also a blessing,
this time in the first person. It was apparently preceded by a messenger formula. It reads, "I bless you through Yahweh of Samaria
(*smrn*) and through his Ashera." Whether *smrn* means "our guard-
ian" or "of Samaria" is disputed. This text is accompanied by the
divine figures already mentioned, which makes it impossible to
understand Asherah here as a cultic place or cultic pole.

The third inscription, from Khirbet el-Qom, comes from a
tomb. It was found next to the stylized image of a hand. The
words are arranged around the drawing without a clear order. The
text probably reads:

Uriyahu, the rich man, wrote it.
Blessed be Uriyahu through Yahweh
for he has saved him from enemies through his Ashera.

By rearranging the middle portion of the text, other scholars find
the inscription to be very similar to the first of those from Kuntillet Ajrud described above. André Lemaire, for example, translates
(p. 44):

Uryahu the wealthy man had it written:
Blessed be Uryahu by Yahweh
and by his Asherah; from his enemies he saved him!

However one chooses to read the three texts, it is difficult to avoid
the impression that a female being is named here alongside Yahweh. The burning question remains: What is meant here by Asherah? Is this the same goddess that we know from the names Baal
and Asherah? During the monarchic period, did worship in Israel
include a pair of deities, in which the pair was Yahweh and the

YAHWEH AND HIS ASHERAH

consort mentioned above, rather than Baal and a corresponding mother-goddess?

There have, of course, been attempts to downplay these inscriptions. Asherah is said to mean not an equal partner of Yahweh, but rather "at most a subordinate helper" (U. Winter, 496) or a holy place (ibid., 552f.). But one cannot get around this so easily. Even a conservative scholar like J. Emerton thinks that though the term Asherah can theoretically refer to a place, since several ancient Near Eastern languages use it in that way, "it is more likely that it denotes a wooden object representing the goddess Asherah" (p. 18). The newly discovered inscriptions are therefore very important for us.

> They confirm what we already knew, namely, that the Asherah was associated with some forms of the cult of Yahweh. The fact that the Asherah is singled out from among other cultic objects to be used alongside the name of Yahweh in blessings at Kuntillet 'Ajrud underlines its special importance in at least one form of popular Yahwism, but otherwise adds nothing of substance to our previous knowledge. The new evidence does not prove that Asherah was regarded in some circles as the consort of Yahweh, though it perhaps strengthens the case for such a view. (Ibid.)

This brief overview shows that the monarchic period did not yet know an exclusive faith in a male God. At least in the provinces and among the common people, the worship of god/goddess pairs and/or of goddesses was known and zealously practiced among the Israelites, the people of Yahweh. It may be that the state religion tolerated behavior that deviated from the Yahwistic norms; it may even have officially practiced a parallel goddess cult here and there (see R. Patai). Conflicts may occasionally have broken out between the state religion and the popular religion. Where does tension not exist between central authority and regional leaders? The authentic words of the classical prophets, primarily Hosea, testify to a sporadic battle against the Baals and Astartes, wood and stone, fertility rites, and the worship of the heavenly multitudes. It is impossible to say where such early exclusive demands for Yahweh came from. It is, however, certain that, in the period of the monarchy, they were weak and rare.

There was apparently no clear instance in which Yahwism was propagated and established as the only permitted faith. The isolated voices of the prophets turned up only rarely. The monarchy was remarkably uninterested in an exclusive worship of Yahweh. The popular religion attended primarily to the well-being of the natural community and was not missionary minded or intolerant. Other champions of a "Yahweh-only movement" (see B. Lang) can only be inferred with difficulty (Elijah?). Even in Israel, the stream of religious traditions included a broad spectrum of ancient Near Eastern ideas and practices. Certainly, these included a female element. The full patriarchal structuring of theology had not yet arrived.

The decisive control question for us, however, is this: Was the status of Israelite women better, freer, and more emancipated in the society of the monarchic period? Can the worship of a god/goddess pair be seen as evidence for the social equality of men and women? Does the worship of both male and female deities have a loosening or liberating effect on a patriarchal society? We can confidently expand this question to include the entire ancient Near East, and we know it retains a certain validity even into the modern period. Unfortunately, both ancient Near Eastern documents and historical experience in general demonstrate no automatic congruence between a people's notions of God or religious values, on the one hand, and their ever-so-human social roles and rankings (with their corresponding privileges or lack thereof) on the other. A patriarchal social order had been operative in the ancient Near East, including Israel, since time immemorial. To be sure, this order was not as blind and inflexible as sometimes described today. Women had their own greater or lesser areas of responsibility. For centuries, however, their responsibilities lay in the narrow framework of the household and child-rearing. Public tasks, including protection of the family and agricultural production, were traditionally reserved for men. These external functions provided men direct access to the spheres of law and religion. Or, stated another way, law and religion, as described in written texts, were essentially public affairs. This gave men primacy both in society and in the family. However, it is important to emphasize that this male priority was normally not based in and did not employ what we would now call sexism. Ancient patriarchy was in actuality a familial order under the management of the man but with inclusion of the woman. At least, that is the simplest way to explain how, in an ancient patriarchal society and religion, female deities were unabashedly worshiped and seen as important and autonomous heavenly agents.

If the return to an all-encompassing goddess and primal mother appears to offer no solution to our problems of social emancipation, might we not try, at least in our churches and our theology, to reinstall a male/female divine pair? Couldn't we promote equal rights for women and men through the worship of a God like "Yahweh and of his Asherah," or the God of Jesus Christ and of the Spirit (envisioned as female)? Reflection and experience make us quite skeptical. Patriarchal theologians in every age have known how to picture a god and goddess in the kind of dependent and dominating relationship that only seems to legitimize the arrogation of human power by men and the subordination and suffering of women. Men have been able to incapacitate queens politically and economically, whether queens of heaven or of earth—just as it has sometimes been possible for women to keep heroes and supermen in line. The liberating potential of sexually differentiated deities is not terribly promising.

On the other hand, radical monotheism might possibly be more inclined to provide the basis for the equality of all people as well as the equality of the sexes. H. Richard Niebuhr pointed to this dimension of faith in his book *Radical Monotheism and Western Culture*, though unfortunately not in relation to the emancipation of women; the time was not yet ripe for this in 1943 (though, in her more recent book, Tikva Frymer-Kensky has made this connection; pp. 213–220). According to Niebuhr, it must eventually dawn on people who confess a single source of life, righteousness, and peace that Blacks, Indians, Jews, Turks, and Vietnamese are also human beings, that the domination of some human beings by others is a mortal sin, that all peoples must cooperate in the shaping and destiny of the earth, and that, as a consequence, women too must find their own personal and civil rights.

4 | *Yahweh, the Tribal Warrior*

Historians agree that before the introduction of the monarchy in the tenth century B.C.E. Israel was organized into clans and tribes. The Old Testament itself remembers the revolutionary transition from tribal rule to centralized monarchy painfully, commenting on it from a variety of perspectives. It was perhaps a contemporary author who wrote the poem, now found in the history of the judges, ridiculing the first attempts to force the separate clans in a given region to subject themselves to royal rule (Judg 9:8–15). After the trees had unsuccessfully summoned the most honored members of their kind (the olive, the fig, and the grape vine) to assume the royal office, they came at last to the bramble, the least valuable and most dangerous plant, saying:

> "You come and reign over us." And the bramble said to the trees, "If in good faith you are anointing me king over you, then come and take refuge in my shade; but if not, let fire come out of the bramble and devour the cedars of Lebanon." (Judg 9:14–15)

This is a wonderfully compact piece of poetry, containing the sharpest imaginable rebuke of sovereign authority. It reveals the self-assurance of independent families and clans, used to living as self-sufficient and self-providing farmers, who were not (or not yet) ready to come together to form a larger and more powerful unit. The memory of their seminomadic history may have played a role in their decision. In Jer 35:1–11, we encounter the clan of Jonadab, son of Rechab, which, around 600 B.C.E. (400 years after the judges), was still tenaciously hanging on to a nomadic way of life with all its rules; clan members rigorously renounced drinking wine, building houses, and cultivating fields.

The late composition of the Deuteronomist includes several levels of commentary on the sometimes turbulent events surrounding the crowning of Saul (1 Samuel 7–11). The Old Testament's testimony is quite clear. Until the time of Saul and David (the beginning of the tenth century B.C.E.), Israel had no king. There had, of course, been city-kings and empire builders for thousands of years in Canaan and in the great river valleys of Mesopotamia and Egypt; but as a relative newcomer to the world of the ancient Near East, Israel maintained its clans and tribes— an earlier form of organizational development—until somewhere around 1000 B.C.E.

Human social development has not followed a simple pattern of linear growth from smaller to larger and more complex social structures. From earliest times to the present, there has been tension between the formation of secondary forms of social organization and the more natural primary forms; the latter have endured or been regularly reconstituted in groups related to family, work, and communal living. Therefore, it would be mistaken to ascribe a greater value to the so-called higher social structures of folk and nation or of various economic and interest groups. On the other hand, the transition from smaller personal groups to larger, anonymous, and more complex communities has certainly played a major role in human history. Differentiation in the means of production and in social roles has produced a disruption and reformation of the "natural" social units. Original prehistoric human society was quite loose—a thin population of independent hordes of hunters and gatherers. Certainly, these groups of Stone Age people were characterized from the beginning by values, norms, roles, and patterns of behavior appropriate to their respective situations as gatherers, hunters, nomadic cattle breeders, fishers, and later also as farmers, before they came together in larger social units. The rise of more or less firmly established large social structures also required theological reflection on the effective radius and power of the deities. But the foundations of human culture and religion date back hundreds of thousands of

years into the early Stone Age, when people still lived together
in small elemental autonomous groups. Even in these prehistoric
times, early contacts and conflicts between the individual groups
produced overlapping relationships and secondary social orders.
The basic human social structure among native peoples on various continents is still the tribe. Within this structure, autonomous clans delegate administrative functions "upward" and provide leaders to fill them. Tribes serve primarily to protect the
family groups and clans they bring together. The social structure
is "segmental," that is, formed of equal but largely independent
units (see C. Sigrist).

But let us return to Israel's premonarchic tribal structure and
its ideas about God. We are talking about the period between
1200 and 1000 b.c.e. It is significant that trustworthy reports
about this phase of Israelite history are very sparse in the Old
Testament. The Old Testament arose in the exilic and postexilic
period as a book of cultic readings and prayers; its collected narratives, songs, proverbs, and rules of behavior were regularly up-
dated. Thus, traces of the prehistory and early history became
blurred and faded. Nevertheless, some essential things of interest
to our investigation remain.

Loosely united clans of seminomads and socially déclassé and
marginalized elements had been settling in the land of Canaan
approximately since the fourteenth century b.c.e., primarily in the
undeveloped and still partially forested mountainous regions between the ancient Canaanite city-states. The new arrivals become
peasant farmers and settled cattle breeders, retaining in their un-
fortified villages their familiar clan structures. However, perhaps
owing to pressure from the rulers of the cities, they joined together in stronger tribal groups. Before long there were tribal
confederations and the first attempts at a concentration of power
among this segment of people who had recently entered the more
developed land. The term they sometimes still used for themselves, "Hebrews" (see Gen 40:15; Exod 1:15, 19), is somehow
related to the *hapiru*, known from ancient Near Eastern sources
as a group of uprooted people often employed by city-dwellers
and kings as day laborers and mercenaries.

The Israelite tribal order was thoroughly patriarchal. Innumerable tribal organizations in Africa, North and South America, and Asia have had a similar male orientation even into recent times. Still today, Muslim Bedouins provide an extreme example of a society dominated by males. In Israel the council of elders—the assembly of clan chiefs—had the deciding voice in the administration of the tribe (see especially W. Thiel, 92–145). The council of elders had a kind of honorary leader, the *nasi'*, comparable to a Bedouin sheik. He had little legislative or executive jurisdiction; at most, he was given certain duties and privileges in times of war. Nevertheless, he must have been highly honored in ancient Israelite society. The oldest collection of laws, the so-called Book of the Covenant, says, for example: "You shall not revile God, or curse a leader [*nasi'*] of your people" (Exod 22:28 [27]). Thus, the tribal leader had divine authority, just as the father and mother participated responsibly in the divine order at the level of the family, at least in the area of child rearing (see Exod 20:12; Lev 19:3). The whole social order had the sanction of the deity, though at the tribal level it seemed to be skewed toward male decision-making. There was no female counterpart to the *nasi'*. Only the male "sheik" had divine privilege. At least in the Old Testament, there was no such office for women.

The situation is somewhat different if we consider another possible "office" within Old Testament tribal society: the so-called judges of the premonarchic period. We have only brief notes, similar to annals, describing the activities of a small group of these leaders. Their role is not easily defined (cf. Judg 10:1–5; 12:7–14). They were apparently the tribal law-keepers and may also have functioned as referees during conflicts among the tribes. But there is also a second category of judges: the great deliverers sent by Yahweh to Israel in times of crisis. Like Gideon and Saul (Judges 6–7; 1 Samuel 10–11), they act under the spontaneous influence of the spirit of God, freeing Israel from a threatening situation. One of these judges, described in ways appropriate to both categories, is a woman, Deborah (Judges 4–5). She was a "prophetess" and judged Israel (Judg 4:4). Without embarrassment, the patriarchal narrator allows a woman to carry out the highest leadership functions in politics and religion. We do not know, of course, how he felt about this, whether it bothered him in the same way that thoughts of a woman president or prime minister might bother some modern western men. At any rate, Deborah is even honored with the title "mother in Israel" (Judg 5:7). On the one hand, she judged Israel sitting under a certain palm (Judg 4:5; cf. Gen 35:8). On the other hand, she also participated in the military and political conflict with the Canaanite city-kings (Judges 4–5). The figure of Deborah simply will not fit in the patriarchal scheme we commonly envision. How was it possible for a woman to assume such decisive roles in a tribal society with such strong male orientation? This historical episode cannot possibly be the invention of later times; given the increasing mistrust of women among succeeding generations, they would never have put a woman in such a visible position. The answer to our question will require us to revise our picture of the ancient patriarchy. Apparently, despite the male leadership of ancient Israelite tribal society, its gender roles were not inherently sexist. In the distribution of domestic duties, the man was given nearly sole responsibility for public and protective functions, as well as for the realms of law and worship. But that did not exclude the possibility that in certain cases women could assume such "male" responsibilities. In any case, the ancient Israelite narrators did not regard women as unable or unsuited to participate in legal and military affairs.

What was the role of religion in the premonarchic tribal society? Were there characteristic notions of the deity that derived from the patriarchal tribal structure? Was Yahweh regarded in that day as male? Following a few general remarks, we will devote ourselves once again to the examination of specific texts.

Faith in God and cultic practice provided cohesion for the ancient Israelite tribes; these factors may, in fact, have been the primary community-building elements. It is probable that the different groups originally worshiped different deities. A later narrator has Joshua, the second great leader of Israel, say, "Long ago your ancestors . . . lived beyond the Euphrates and served other gods" (Josh 24:2). These words correctly remember the polytheistic past of the pre-Israelite groups. Even the name "Israel" is a compound of "El," the common Canaanite word for god, rather than a combining form of "Yahweh," the later national deity.

But the God Yahweh does appear on the scene of religious history during those centuries and begins to establish himself in Israel's tribal society, gradually achieving priority status. Most likely, sometime around 1200 B.C.E., a new group of seminomads, often called the Moses group, joined itself to the tribes then coming together in Canaan; this group brought with it the worship of the God Yahweh, either from the Sinai Peninsula or from the region east of the Jordan. These people told of their miraculous deliverance by Yahweh from a group of Egyptian chariots. "Sing to Yahweh, for he has triumphed gloriously; horse and rider he has thrown into the sea" (Exod 15:21). The religious experience lying behind this joyful confession had a lasting effect on the circle of Israelite peasants; in fact, it became decisive for the entire religious history of Israel and has marked world history as well. Its effects continue in the Judeo-Christian tradition, and it has even left its traces in events like the German struggle for liberation from Napoleon ("The LORD defeated him—horse, rider, and wagon") and the often bloody conflicts involving the redistribution of land in Latin America. For ancient Israel, the deliverance of Moses and his followers at the Sea of Reeds was of particular importance because it raised the possibility of similar victories within the land of Canaan itself. The Canaanite city-states had become dangerous opponents of the tribal peasants and shepherds, but Yahweh, the God who came from afar, hurrying to the aid of his devotees from Sinai (Judg 5:5; Ps 68:8 [9]) or from the mountains of Seir (Judg 5:4) or Mount Paran (Hab 3:3), proved superior in the conflicts with the more culturally developed and better equipped Canaanites. This mountain deity, unknown to Canaan but a covenantal partner of the increasingly powerful Israelite tribes, induced more and more fear among the older inhabitants of the land (see, for example, the later reference in 1 Kgs 20:23: "[Israel's] gods are gods of the hills, and so they were stronger than we").

Under these circumstances, it is not surprising that faith in Yahweh became the most important identifying characteristic of the Israelite tribes. At first, this tribal deity may still have been worshiped at his original location in the south or to the east of the land of Canaan (see 1 Kgs 19:8), but later he was also worshiped in sanctuaries in the newly settled areas. We learn, for example, of cultic centers for Yahweh at Shechem, Gilgal, Shiloh, and other Israelite sites. The usual occasion for Yahweh worship was probably seasonal pilgrimage festivals (see 1 Sam 1:3) or special days of remembrance for liberation from foreign rule and oppression. Entire families participated in such religious celebrations, as we see clearly in the story of Hannah and Elkanah (1 Sam 1). But we need to understand that the Yahweh cult functioned at the level of the tribe or perhaps tribal confederation. Beneath this sociopolitical level, within families and clans, other religious forms prevailed; these were to some degree made Yahwistic (as some groups of Psalms show), but they retained their own distinct profile. Certainly, during Israel's tribal period, Yahweh worship kept the single male deity firmly in the foreground, but it did not in principle exclude the worship of other deities along with him. Viewed from the perspective of the history of religions, the saving god always was afforded priority in the worship life of his followers. The trouble is that since the sources from Israel's tribal period are so sparse, we can say nothing at all about tribal deities other than Yahweh. The question about a possible female partner for Yahweh (comparable to the situation with Chemosh and Milcom among the Moabites and Ammonites) must also go unanswered.

We can say provisionally that in the premonarchic period Israelite society was clearly organized in several layers. The important base, both for the life of the individual and of the superimposed institutions, was the extended family. It was largely autonomous—economically, legally, and, most likely, in matters of religion as well (though more about that later). The superimposed tribal formation had its own specific functions, particularly in maintaining the legal system, providing for defense, and cultic worship. But this premonarchic secondary social structure did not yet contain elements of centralized government. It would scarcely have been possible to use compulsion to enforce the will of the tribal organization above the extended family. The tribal war against Benjamin in Judges 20 is a highly stylized later exception. At the level of the tribe or tribal confederations, participants cooperated voluntarily and consensually in their own self-interest (see Judg 5). The elders, that is, the heads of the families, maintained parity among themselves. The leader of the tribe (*nasi'*) was, at most, *primus inter pares*. It was only in time of war that a person seized by the spirit of Yahweh was occasionally recognized as commander-in-chief with God-given power to command obedience. The primary element linking all aspects of the tribal organization was the Yahweh cult. But it had little to do with domestic religious practice, even though the entire family regularly participated in the cultic celebrations. If one element of Israelite society could rightly be called patriarchal (male dominated), it would have to be the tribal organization. The areas of responsibility covered by the tribe—law and warfare—were almost solely reserved for men. Consequently, cultic practice at this level also lay in the hands of men. Women, children, and slaves participated in the rites as members of the patriarchal family.

It is, therefore, all the more surprising that women play an extraordinarily important role in two songs of war and victory, both of which are apparently quite old and close to the original events. Is this only because the Israelite peasant farmers were living in a pioneer situation? We know, for example, that in the white conquest of the American continent women often had to assume roles normally reserved for men. Or might there have been theological reasons for the remarkable importance of women in the defensive battles of early Israel? We need to examine the texts.

Form-critically, the Song of Deborah (Judges 5) is an early Israelite victory song. Often including concrete details, exaggerated descriptions, and archaic religious language and images, the song tells of the decisive battle of an Israelite tribe against a modernly equipped force of Canaanite chariots. Thanks to the overpowering intervention of Yahweh, the Israelites (who were, after all, farmers fighting on foot, most likely with primitive weapons) were able to defeat the chariot forces of the Canaanite mercenaries decisively. Sisera, the fleeing commander of the Canaanite coalition, was killed by the woman Jael while in the tent of a Kenite family that was apparently friendly to the Israelite tribes.

What does this victory song tell us about God? Yahweh, a God foreign to Canaan, appears from the Edomite wilderness or from Sinai, accompanied by a terrifying display of the forces of nature. The earth quakes, the mountains (thought to be pillars holding up the world) shake, and rain falls in torrents (Judg 5:4–5). These are typical signs of a mighty theophany (see J. Jeremias). They accompany the appearance of a weather-god or war-god. In addition to the shaking earth and tumultuous floods, the texts frequently also mention fire and storms among the natural forces (cf. Ps 18:7–15 [8–16]; 50:2–3; 97:2–5). Is this an inherently male description of the appearance of the deity? Is it some kind of sexist male display behavior? The text certainly makes no direct reference to any such notion. The turmoil of the primal forces should be understood as a reaction of terror on the part of nature and a demonstration of humility before the powerful god of war. But these natural forces cannot simply be identified with the female principle or a primal female deity. Such a sexist interpretation would be out of place even applied to the Babylonian creation myth, in which the primal mother Tiamat is defeated and cut into pieces. None of the chaos myths are about a conflict between male and female elements. In both the ancient Near East and the Old Testament, the overthrow of the powers of chaos by the saving god who comes in answer to the people's cry is not about the elimination of something essentially female; it describes the containment and overthrow of life-threatening evil itself, the pacification of the world, liberation from the danger of death. Evil is in no way understood as female, even though, under the influence of sharply dualistic thought, some later strands of tradition will develop a tendency in that direction (see the "woman sitting in the basket" in Zech 5:5–11). On the other hand, it is both noteworthy and peculiar that in our text a tribal God such as Yahweh is associated with cosmic or mythic ideas that come from the more developed cultures.

Yahweh is unequivocally and emphatically the "God of Israel," and Israel is the "people of God" (Judg 5:3, 5, 11). The tribal deity stands in solidarity with his adherents and is just as strongly related to them as are all national or state deities. The god or goddess is a member and leader of the group and sides completely with these people. In those days, every war was also a war between the gods and goddesses associated with the groups in question. The inscription of King Mesha, already cited, sets Chemosh, the national god of the Moabites, against Yahweh, the God of the Is-

raelites. Assyrian and Babylonian victory inscriptions ascribe both
the call to war and the final victory to their gods, Ashur or Marduk. "I fought with them with the support of the mighty forces of
Ashur, which Ashur, my lord, has given to me, and the strong
weapons which Nergal, my leader, has presented to me," says the
Assyrian King Shalmaneser III after his victory over an Israelite-
Canaanite coalition in ca. 855 B.C.E. (Pritchard, 279). After a victory at Megiddo over a Syrian-Canaanite coalition (1468 B.C.E.),
Pharaoh Thut-mose III celebrated the event with these words on
the wall of a temple at Karnak in Egypt:

> May ye give praise to [Amon]; may ye extol the might of his majesty,
> because his arm is greater than that of any king. . . . Then the entire
> army rejoiced and gave praise to Amon because of the victory which
> he had given to his son on this day. They lauded his majesty and ex-
> tolled his victories. Then they presented the plunder which they had
> taken. (Pritchard, 236–237)

A tribal deity like Yahweh is also obligated to take the field against
the enemies of his adherents or to stand up for his own people
against other peoples and their gods. "So perish all your enemies,
O LORD! But may your friends be like the sun as it rises in its
might" (Judg 5:31). This sentence is probably a later addition to
the victory song, given its prosaic generalization. Nevertheless, it
fully agrees in content with the flow of the entire song and with
the old saying associated with the ark: "Arise, O LORD, let your
enemies be scattered, and your foes flee before you" (Num 10:35).
Many passages in the Old Testament speak of Yahweh's intervention against the enemies (see, for example, Pss 68:1–3 [2–4]; 91;
Habakkuk 3; Isa 59:15–21; 63:1–6). In the ancient Near East, it
was not only male gods who assumed the role of warring deities
fighting for their people. Inanna and Ishtar intervene in the same
way for their kings and subjects. Such behavior is also associated
with the goddess Anat in Canaan, who, in conflicts with her enemies, wades ankle-deep in blood. I also find it significant that the
ancient Near Eastern victory songs often ascribe the victory to a
single god, though this, of course, says nothing about the presence or absence of other deities among the people in question.

Further, the role of war-god is in no way reserved exclusively for male deities.

Israel is the people of Yahweh, and according to our victory song this entails a variety of obligations. First among them is fidelity in their devotion to Yahweh (Judg 5:2, 9, 13) and unconditional solidarity with one another. In vv. 13–18, several tribes are called to join Yahweh in battle. Ephraim, Benjamin, Machir, Zebulun, Issachar, and Naphtali are praised for their faithful devotion. Reuben, Gilead, Asher, Dan, and the city of Meroz are severely criticized for failing to participate in Yahweh's war. We see that the duty to fight was a prominent feature of the collection of tribes that called itself Israel, and this observation gives us some insight into the nature of Yahweh. He was the protector and war-god of the tribes of Israel. We know little of any other functions. Consequently, Yahweh comes to Israel's aid. He apparently commands both the forces of heaven and the powers of the deep: "The stars fought from heaven . . ." (Judg 5:20). Sisera's troops are powerless against such force. "The torrent Kishon swept them away, the onrushing torrent, the torrent Kishon" (Judg 5:21). This verse is an allusion to the primeval flood, the waters of chaos. Again, associating all these various powers with a tribal deity is highly improbable; in the myths of the surrounding peoples the different powers are strictly limited to particular gods and goddesses. Even though there are occasional exceptions, deities are almost always associated either with the heavens or the earth. It is possible that the title "Yahweh Sabaoth," which occurs more than two hundred times in the Old Testament, means to encompass both: Yahweh rules in the upper regions and is also able to repel the powers of the underworld. In any event, according to Judges 5, faith in this powerful mountain God, who is superior to the gods of the more developed lands, constitutes the fundamental confession of the tribal society.

Yahweh's male gender is not expressly mentioned in the Song of Deborah, and, at the same time, the women Deborah and Jael are the primary actors in this hymn. Yahweh fights alone in the battle. According to their victory inscriptions, the ancient Near Eastern religions also ascribed the burden of battle to the deity. Generally, a male deity acted as war-god and savior. It was more an exception for a goddess to participate in battle, although in the heavenly pantheon they would scarcely be burdened with housework, field work, or child-rearing. The distribution of roles among the deities reflects the human scene and division of labor. So it is no surprise that the tribal God of Israel, Yahweh, is also portrayed as a male warrior. The casual naming of the goddess Anath in Judg 5:6 is not meant to emphasize Yahweh's gender or point to her as a possible partner in battle. But the song's strong emphasis on the two women is, in fact, startling. Deborah is not only the singer of the victory song ("I will make melody to the LORD . . . "; Judg 5:3), but also the one who inspires and apparently leads the battle (Judg 5:7; 4:8–9). And despite the levy of so many tribes, Jael is the only one who enters the action as a covenant partner of Yahweh and actually carries out a decisive act of liberation (Judg 5:24–27). The activity of the men, according to the song, seems to be have been limited to hesitantly and reluctantly following Deborah's call to arms and, at the end, dividing the booty among themselves (Judg 5:30). In fact, Judges 5 portrays women in such a prominent role in Israel's decisive battle against the Canaanites that one can rightly ask whether, at that time, the whole Yahweh religion was primarily a woman's affair. For reasons already cited, this is, of course, improbable. But the victory song clearly demonstrates that women were fully integrated into tribal society. Nevertheless, that society was defined by patriarchy. Even Deborah is introduced as the wife of Lappidoth (Judg 4:4). She was regarded as an ordinary member of a clan with patrilinear structure. But the affiliation with her husband and his family did not prevent a woman, in exceptional cases, from assuming responsibilities normally reserved for men. Patriarchal jargon would say that, within tribal society, women could "act like a man," more or less without hindrance, when the need arose. The narrator of Judges 4 even ridicules the cowardly men. For him, Deborah is a model of "male" decisiveness and action. This detail also demonstrates the unbiased coexistence of the sexes in their different roles. In time of war early Israelite women had the important task of supplying provisions and moral support to the warriors and, above all, of appropriately honoring the victors when they returned home. According to established custom, they went out to meet the returning heros and sang the first hymns of praise (1 Sam 18:6–7; Judg 11:34). The heroic deeds, reported by the women in stirring detail, served primarily in the patriarchal society to encourage the tired warriors (see the books of Esther and Judith). Despite everything, in the developmental stages of Israel—the time of the tribal society—there was apparently a relative balance between the various areas of responsibility of the two sexes within the overall patriarchal order.

The same thing is confirmed by the second important text from that era. Again, we are dealing with a victory song, this one sung by "the prophet Miriam, Aaron's sister" and other women after the Egyptian chariots had sunk in the Sea of Reeds (Exod 15:20–21). Apparently, a later scribe gives her the title prophet (as in Judg 4:4) to try to legitimize this woman who dared open her mouth in holy affairs. In an earlier period, women required no such legitimation. The verse sung by Miriam, which was then probably repeated endlessly, is unparalleled song of praise to the saving God Yahweh. Here, too, we see that the narrator envisions a close trusting relationship between women and Israel's male tribal deity. Further, it is particularly interesting that Miriam is not only called the sister of two of the highest leaders of Israel, but is also made a kind of female antagonist of Moses in matters of religious equal rights (Num 12:1–15). Might this account retain memories of an original indigenous religion of women or the worship of goddesses in Israel? That is possible, but the text contains several layers and contradictions, making it difficult to determine the actual issue at stake. Is it a matter of recognizing the mediating function of the prophet over against the established leadership of the congregation (Num 12:2, 6–8)? Is it a question of rival groups of descendants taking shelter behind the names Miriam, Aaron, and Moses in their claims to congregational leadership? Whatever the case may be, the song of Miriam and its echoes in the literature of the Old Testament demonstrate the unabashed worship of Yahweh by prominent Israelite women of the early period (see R. Burns). Both the song and story of Miriam show that early Israelite women were not reduced to second-class status.

Since the evidence from the Israelite tribal era is so meager, it will be advantageous to seek other sources of information. Happily, since the beginning of this century, anthropologists have studied countless existing tribal societies. Some of the fundamental conditions of religious life brought to light by those studies can provide at least some sense of the background for the tribal religion of ancient Israel. This comparison is not meant to prejudge the details of the Israelite experience of faith, of their cultic ceremonies or theological perspectives. Nevertheless, a fuller understanding of tribal organizations accessible to us through anthropology and sociology will be of great help in properly classifying the few witnesses to the tribal period in the Old Testament.

In our century, anthropological field studies of tribal societies have been undertaken in great number on every continent. As a rule, and this is an important innovation in scientific anthropology, the researchers lived for some time among the indigenous peoples in order to comprehend their social and religious systems from within. The anthropologists were interested chiefly in the tribal systems of kinship and interaction, the flow of production and economics, and the political structures and world of thought. Increasingly, however, religion became recognized as an integral part of these so-called "primitive" societies and included in the investigations. Since Emile Durkheim attempted a synthesis of the then known facts in his epoch-making work, *The Elementary Forms of the Religious Life* (French original, 1912), there has been a nearly incomprehensible wealth of empirical studies in many countries. For example, the religious world of the South Sea Islanders has been studied by B. Malinowski, R. F. Fortune, M. Mead, and R. Firth. E. E. Evans-Pritchard, G. Lienhardt, and J. Middleton lived among the Sudanese tribes. V. W. Turner described the rites of groups in Central Africa. Latin America produced important anthropologists of religion such as B. D. Ribeiro and the Vilas-Boas brothers. North America has become a stronghold of empirical social anthropology and the investigation of tribal religions. I mention here only C. Kluckhohn, R. Benedict, and R. Underhill. North American scholars also relatively quickly produced theoretical summaries of what had been learned in field studies about the religion of the so-called primitive peoples. Among these were the works of E. O. James (1917), R. H. Lowie

(1925), B. Radin (1938), W. J. Goode (1951), and G. Swanson (1960). This great abundance of data can, for our purposes, be summarized in the following points:

1. Almost everywhere, the tasks of daily life are carefully divided between the sexes. The man is responsible for public appearances and the work away from the home. He fulfills protective functions and assumes a portion of the field work and the care of the flocks. The woman has responsibility for the children, the household, food preparation, and for a major part of the manual labor in and around the house (care of small animals and garden). There is some fluctuation in the assignment of external duties.

2. The spheres associated with the sexes remain strictly separate. Male and female domains are mutually taboo. Women dare not touch the men's hunting weapons; menstruation and birth bring great danger to men.

3. There is generally a balance in sexual and personal relationships. Primary decision-making in household affairs can be assumed by either one side or the other, by the woman or the man. Representing the family in public is usually a male duty. That does not change under matrilinear family and clan structures.

4. In religious affairs, many ceremonies bring the clan together. On those occasions, men and women participate in different functions. Very frequently there are independent rites for women and for men (Hopi Indians, for example, have separate ceremonial areas).

5. The common religious life of the village or tribe stands above the familial cult. The larger social unit either develops its own rites, festivals, and celebrations, or its religious affairs are incorporated into the familial celebrations.

6. A very large number of deities, divine beings, demons, spirits, and powers play a role in tribal religions. Nowhere does their sexual differentiation seem to be an issue. Tribal religions know both sexual and asexual deities.

7. Normally, a ritual expert, shaman, or priest is authoritatively involved in religious rites that extend beyond the familial framework. This specialist is occasionally also drawn into more intimate religious acts, but his actual field of activity is the higher level of the clan and tribe. At this level there is almost never a

female spiritual leader. Tribal religion is normally under the control of men.

8. Healing the sick usually takes place in the household. The annual cycles of planting, harvesting, hunting, and migration provide the occasion for the practice of the higher tribal religion. In addition, the tribal religion controls the ceremonies of war and victory.

9. The polarity of the sexes is visible in many of the religious rituals. Sometimes it determines the basic structure of the ceremony (cf. V. Turner). Teasing between men and women, verbal competitions, praise or ridicule of one's own or the opposite sex, and exaggerated descriptions and portrayals of sexual characteristics are a part of many religious celebrations.

10. Among tribal societies, women almost always have an attendant function in war ceremonies. For example, according to the eye-witness testimony of a mercenary from Hesse in the Portuguese military service, Tupinambá women are responsible for watching over, supplying, ritualistically deriding, and feeding prisoners of war (H. Staden).

In summary, tribal religions are generally led by men. Their understanding of God corresponds to the protective and warrior functions defined by the tribe. But the female element is included in a polar fashion (Y. Murphy and R. F. Murphy).

This review of tribal culture leads to the conclusion that a patriarchal structure in church and public affairs is outmoded today. If patriarchal tribal society already ascribes a bipolar structure to public responsibility and allows women an attendant role even in the most innately male domain, that is, the protection of the family against external enemies, how much more must our contemporary social order, with its legal, ethical, and religious sensibilities, give equal responsibility to women and men in shaping public and ecclesiastical life. In an industrial society women and men are thrown together, theoretically and practically, in education and politics, in economics and law. For decades, social life as we know it has only been made possible by the common work of both sexes. The dominance of men, solely on the basis of their gender, was understandable in earlier times because of the contemporary forms of life and work; but it has no justification whatever in today's society. Both theology and church also depend today upon the equal participation of women and men (cf. chapter 8). The tribal deity Yahweh never in principle excluded women from his cult. Given his well-known fairness and solidarity with both male and female followers, a stance that produced an equivalent obligation of solidarity among human beings, this same Yahweh would certainly demand today the full equality of women and men.

5 | Women and the Domestic Cult

If it is hard to define the contours of the official faith and religion of the national and prenational periods, it will be even more difficult to discover the religious practices within the family unit. Only seldom do everyday affairs and women's realities find their way into a literature devoted to the male world of external affairs. But one thing can be said with certainty: the deity was worshiped also at the family level in ancient Israel. Men set the predominant tone in religious and cultic matters in the higher secondary forms of social organization. This is to be expected, given the social division of labor that ascribed the responsibility for the family's external matters to the man and its domestic responsibilities to the woman. But what can be said about religious activities within the family circle? The dearth of direct witnesses to domestic religious ceremonies dare not keep us from inquiring about a possible distribution of roles based on gender. What we would like to know is whether and how Israelite women participated in the worship of God in the innermost family circle.

The first impressions, which will be further examined in chapter 6, are not especially encouraging for women. The oldest form of Israelite religion related to the extended family appears to be completely male-centered. Since the work of Albrecht Alt, the literature has described this form as the seminomadic religion of the fathers. This impression is contradicted, however, by the late witness of Jeremiah 44: we have seen that in the sixth century there were traces of a female-led goddess worship in which men and children supported the mothers, who bore the primary responsibility. Since this custom is known in Jerusalem as late as the

55

sixth century, must it not have been a regular feature of the more open national and prenational society?

Again, we will investigate Old Testament texts, paying attention to recent interpretations of the biblical material. The professional literature has focused almost exclusively on the historical development of Israel's official cult; in considering women, it has referred, above all, to their participation in services of reading and preaching after the exile (see Deut 31:10–13; Jer 44:15; Josh 8:35; Ezra 10:1; Neh 8:2). All these passages speak about the whole Israelite congregation, demonstrating nothing more than that men, women, children (to some degree), foreigners, and others had a right to be present at worship and the accompanying festivities. If the texts point to any division within the congregation, it is not between the sexes but between the priests and Levites, on one side, and the laity, who passively experience the readings, prayers, and preaching, on the other.

People have also referred to the prayer of Hannah in 1 Samuel 1–2 and to the prophetesses Huldah (2 Kgs 22:13–14), Miriam (Exod 15:20), Deborah (Judg 4:4), Noadiah (Neh 6:14), and the anonymous Israelite women in Ezek 13:17 who "prophesy out of their own imagination," that is, who speak in the name of a deity on their own authority, allegedly without a commission. In addition, they are accused of practicing magic (v. 18). Insofar as these texts refer to activities regarded as positive, the women in question find a certain place at the margins of the official cult. They were allowed to pray, but probably only at some distance from the holy of holies. Prophecy derives from a verbal gift that is not easily regulated by the priests and the religious establishment. Joel 3:1–5, for example, speaks of the pouring out of the Spirit on both male and female members of the people of God. Thus, none of these texts prove that women themselves had public dealings with the holy realm. The texts do not connect women with altar, temple, sacrificial animals, idols, steles, or holy vessels. The closest thing to cultic activity in its ancient sense are the strange references in Exod 38:8 and 1 Sam 2:22, according to which women "served at the entrance to the tent of meeting." Apparently they did something with sacred mirrors. Israelite women probably never came closer than this to the official temple of Yahweh.

More important for our investigation into the domestic cult are the passages in the Old Testament that accuse women of independent religious activity in the service of other deities. Ezek 13:17–19 is one example. Another is the story of the necromancer of Endor (1 Samuel 28). In this and similar texts, women are seen as subversive agents, working against the religion of Yahweh. Their religious activity is so strongly stigmatized—indeed, pushed into the zone of things terrible, forbidden, and dangerous—that the actual features of their cultic practice are no longer recognizable. (The stigma remains to the present day: many women's groups, especially in the United States, believe their only option is some kind of counter-Christian religious practice or even Satanism.) But one can legitimately ask whether the proscribed cultic practices found here and there in the Old Testament might not conceal an original genuine female or domestic cult.

The extensive list of forbidden practices in Deut 18:10–11 does not assume female wrongdoers. The acts of divination and conjuring named there, some of which are more fully known to us from ancient Near Eastern sources, are ascribed to men, as they are in several other passages (see, for example, 2 Kgs 21:6; Mal 3:5). At the most, women are included along with men in the text's masculine verbal and nominal grammatical forms. Other passages, however, do seem to come close to voicing particular mistrust of an independent female religiosity. Exod 22:18 [17], for example, in a list of death threats for capital offenses, commands: "You shall not permit a female sorcerer to live." There is no corresponding regulation against male sorcerers, even though the following two sentences speak of male wrongdoers. In the figurative language of Isa 57:3, the Israelites are called "children of a sorceress," and texts already mentioned (Ezek 13:17–19, 1 Samuel 28) aim their accusations of underground religious activity particularly at women. Such texts reflect traditions that suspected women of being carriers of deviant religious notions (see chapter 7). Whether we can postulate a female domestic and familial cult on the basis of these texts remains doubtful at best. All societies proscribe magic practices seen as dangerous to the group (which anthropology has often called "black" magic). Viewed as a whole, Old Testament texts regard men and women equally susceptible to such dark cultic practices. Although magic, divination, and conjuring occasionally come into contact with the official state and temple religion, their roots are actually to be found in popular religiosity. Women clearly have a much more active role at this level than in the official cultic activity of the tribe or state—a fact important to our investigation. Nevertheless, the cultic practices described in these texts are hardly imaginable within families. The male and female sorcerers, which later Old Testament writers sought to eliminate from Israel, were specialists in performing ritual acts on behalf of individuals, similar to miraculous healers of our day. They hired themselves out to a regional clientele. At the most, they would have come in from the outside for sporadic participation in our postulated domestic cult (see 1 Sam 28:7; 2 Kgs 4:21–22).

There are Old Testament texts other than Jeremiah 44, however, that suggest (though indirectly) that women bore joint or even sole responsibility for divine worship in the religion of the family or clan—more precisely, in the domestic cult. One very ancient reference fits erratically in the Moses narrative. During the family's "flight into Egypt" (Exod 4:25), Zipporah circumcises her son (or is it really her husband or son-in-law?). It is unheard of for a woman to carry out a blood rite. This story could never have been invented at a later date, because the separation of women from the official sacrificial cult was practiced with increasing rigor. The cry "You are a bridegroom of blood to me" (v. 25) is surely an ancient cultic formula. The clumsy later explanation in v. 26 ("At that time [one] said 'bridegroom of blood' [in reference] to circumcision," NIV [alt.]) shows only that, very early on, people could not make sense of the custom portrayed in this text or sought to suppress it. In and of itself, the bridegroom-of-blood formula is a sign of the acceptance of a son-in-law into his wife's family circle. Since the sentence "You are a bridegroom of blood to me" can logically be spoken only by a wife or her mother, it is the only direct evidence of a responsible participation by women in the innermost cultic activity. The formula refers to becoming related through marriage. Consequently, it belongs to a familial or interfamilial cultic act.

But there is also indirect evidence of the existence of a domes-

tic cult in early Israel. Most important are the references to teraphim. These are cultic objects that, at least in some cases, must
be seen as household idols. According to the contractual arrange-
ment described in Exod 21:6, the partners appear before an idol
that is apparently placed in a niche near the entrance to the house.
In this case, it is the head of the family who performs the brief
cultic ceremony. In other references, however, women frequently
have remarkably close contact with the divine image. If Michal,
Rachel, and perhaps Miriam had not had some real connection to
cultic life, the stories about them would hardly have arisen. Or
is every reference to a woman's contact with teraphim meant to
condemn the worship of foreign, non-Yahwistic deities?

Let us first examine the texts and the situations they describe.
In Gen 31:14–42, Jacob and his family flee from Mesopotamia
and thereby come into conflict with his uncle (or cousin) and employer, Laban (the "Aramean"). Interwoven in this story, among
all its conflicts, is a dramatic feature relating to the worship of
household gods. Rachel, Jacob's favorite wife and the younger
daughter of Laban, and Leah, Rachel's older sister, support the
secret departure from their home because their father had deceived them. "Is there any portion or inheritance left to us in our
father's house? Are we not regarded by him as foreigners? For he
has sold us, and he has been using up the money given for us"
(Gen 31:14–15). The reader needs to know that the so-called
bride price, given by the groom or his family to the father of the
bride, remained entirely or in part with the bride's father, in case
the woman was put away by her husband and had to return home.
In the view of some scholars of the ancient Near East, among
some west Semitic peoples, and even in Babylon under Hammurapi, this bride money was given by the father to the daughter for
her own safekeeping as a kind of insurance. (References to the
western Semitic practice are found in Ugarit, Mari, Nuzi, and
Alalakh). Apparently in retribution for her father's embezzlement,
Rachel steals the "household gods," that is, the teraphim of her
father Laban. What exactly are the teraphim that turn up here in
the family cult? The term can refer to various objects used in cultic worship, including the small figurines or statues of deities
found in various forms (mostly female) in almost all Canaanite or

Syrian excavations, to the larger cultic images that require their own chapel, and possibly to cultic masks. The traditional etymologies, most of which give a singular meaning to the plural form, are of little value and probably untenable. The most likely proposal is that teraphim is a Hurrian loan word that means something like demon or protecting spirit. Hurrian texts refer to a pair of protecting deities under the names *tarpis* and *annaris*, similar to the Babylonian deities *lamassu* and *sedu*. The Hurrians, who were neither Semites nor Indo-Europeans, ruled Syria and Canaan from the Caucasus Mountains during the first half of the second millennium B.C.E. They left their mark on the proto-Israelite population and language, as well as on its patterns of thought and belief (even though the hypothetical reconstructions based on the often striking agreement in custom and practice between the Old Testament and the Nuzi texts are sometimes exaggerated). Thus, I find the recent etymological derivation of the word *teraphim* form *tarpis* (protecting deity) to be the most likely. The related notion of the "personal god," so important in Babylonian religion, will be taken up below.

If teraphim means something like protecting deity or household god, the story in Genesis 31 makes good sense and allows us to deduce the function of the cultic image. In this case, the image is rather small, since it is easily concealed under the saddle of a camel. Laban is dismayed over the loss of *his* household deity. His family's good fortune is at stake. He threatens the thief with death. This is fully acceptable to Jacob, who knows nothing of the actual events. The clever young daughter of Laban was the thief, seeking to square accounts with her father. It is not clear whether her taking the gods from her father's household might also have brought a claim to an inheritance or even to his entire property. Presumably, she steals only the benign spirit, the guarantor of good fortune. The fact that she does this on her own, taking the risk of being discovered—that she pursues her own claims and rights—allows us to assume that the administration of the ancient Israelite household was at least in part a woman's affair. One must also wonder about Rachel's lack of respect in handling the cultic image. She does not shy away from putting it under the camel's saddle and sitting on it. Later Jewish readers would certainly have seen this as a terrible desecration, an affront to the image—perhaps a well-deserved profanation of an idol. Rachel pretends that "the way of women" is upon her. Late priestly circles did, indeed, regard menstrual blood as altogether unclean. The touch of a menstruating woman made objects and people cultically unfit. But if this story predates the fully developed priestly theology of cleanness, then we need not read it through priestly glasses. In tribal societies and domestic cultures one often treats holy things quite roughly. Anthropologists report that idols are sometimes slapped. Hesitation to make direct contact with the sacred, abstract notions of the deity, and the fear of profane encounters with idols develop only with a growing sense of divine transcendence and the extension of taboo zones. However we evaluate the Rachel tradition, one thing is sure: a woman handles cultic objects with complete self-confidence. She has her own interest in them and lays claim to an inherent right.

The second story in which teraphim play an important role is told in the book of Judges. According to Judges 17–18, a woman commissions the production of ephod and teraphim or, in another level of the tradition, of a carved and cast image of a deity. The care of the image and the cultic activity that no doubt accompanied it were given over to the woman's grandson and later to a professional Levitical priest. In the text discussed above, Exod 21:6, as well as in 1 Sam 15:23; 2 Kgs 23:24; and Ezek 21:26, only men deal with cultic objects. The references in Hos 3:4 and Zech 10:2 are unclear because they refer to the entire people. In any event, one can hear in all these texts the clear opinion of the later authors that teraphim had something to do with soothsaying or oracles. And though ancient Near Eastern kings tried to learn the fate of their official decisions and undertakings, it is certain that the art of soothsaying had its original home among everyday people, where it served the mastery of personal life. We should not be led astray by the references to male prerogatives in relation to the teraphim, for we have another important text that brings a woman into contact with this cultic object. Michal, Saul's daughter, handles the teraphim in her house. She uses the teraphim as a doll, simulating a sleeping David, so her father's bailiffs are temporarily deceived (1 Sam 19:13: "Michal took an idol and laid it on the bed; she put a net of goats' hair on its head, and covered it with the clothes"). On the basis of this account, commentators speculate that Michal's teraphim must have been larger than a figurine and must have had human features, that is, that it was a kind of cultic statue or mask. This argument is not altogether convincing. It is very easy to simulate a human figure by, say, using the fold of a blanket with carefully placed goat hair emerging from it. No particularly large figure is required. We tried such things as students. A small bust of Shakespeare was enough to frighten away a colleague in confusion, thinking his bed was already being used. And when Michal used the relatively small household god as a dummy for David, she no doubt trusted it to mislead the pursuers because it had, after all, divine capacities. In any event, Michal makes cunning and bold use of the idol. Does the narrator see her as a "mere" housewife, exercising only a passive relationship to the image and its cult? The reported events seem to suggest otherwise.

Another indicator of the strong place of women in the religion of the ancient Israelite family are the many passages in which "father and mother"—and once, emphatically, "mother and father" (Lev 19:3)—are named together as equal authorities in relation to the children (or sons). This usage is firmly anchored in the wisdom texts. Both parents give instruction in ethical living to their offspring and are thereby preservers of the sacred tradition (see Prov 1:8–9; 6:20–23; 23:22; 31:1). So it is no surprise that both parents stand under the special protection of the deity. Children should "honor" (Exod 20:12) or "respect" (Lev 19:3) their father and mother. Anyone who offends against this command born of the family ethos—anyone who, for example, even strikes or curses their father and mother—is strictly punished (see Prov 30:17; Exod 21:15, 17; Deut 21:18–21). The commandment to honor the parents and the prohibition against cursing them show the deep religious significance of the parent-child relationship. In this sense, the father and mother are equal to the tribal chief (Exod 22:28 [27]) or the king (1 Kgs 21:10; Eccl 10:20). Like them, parents enjoy divine immunity as guarantors of social order. Only God himself is similarly unassailable. Human beings compared so directly to God must certainly have had cultic functions and roles.

Unfortunately, there are no more precise reports to make clear that women were responsible for the family god(s) within the household. The only evidence (which taken by itself would not be sufficient) is the accusation in Jeremiah that apostate Israelites, under the leadership of the mothers, offered sacrifices to the queen of heaven in Jerusalem and later in Egypt (Jer 44:15–19; see chapter 2 in this book). Some other Old Testament passages seem to speak of a private cult on the flat roof of the house (Jer 19:13; 32:29; 2 Kgs 23:12; Zeph 1:5). The details of the ritual are, however, not reported. The texts speak only of the worship of the host of heaven or Baal, and of libations to "other gods." But we learn nothing about who was responsible for leading these ceremonies. Thus, we can speak only of the probability of a domestic or familial cult in premonarchic Israel. It is difficult to say more about the initiative or responsibility of women. But the limitation is inherent, since our sources have preserved relatively little data about intimate familial affairs.

Examining Israel's neighboring religions is also not terribly helpful. For one thing, the sources are minimal, just as they are in the Old Testament. The tradition has maintained primarily reports about the official religion. But the religion of larger societies was normally controlled by men, even where goddesses were being worshiped. The division of labor into gender-specific external and internal functions was also practiced among Israel's neighboring cultures and societies. Second, the tremendous cultural and social differences between premonarchic Israel and the highly developed neighboring states permits us to draw analogies only with considerable caution. Third, research into the role of women is not highly developed in this area. The family cult has also been neglected in ancient Near Eastern research (see B. Menzel; J. Ochshorn; D. Wolkstein). Nevertheless, at least a few investigations of private documents deserve mention. In 1971, Willem Römer published a study of selected texts from Mari (*Frauenbriefe über Religion, Politik und Privatleben in Mari*). These texts, preserved on clay tablets, were all written (or dictated?) by women of the royal court. Most are addressed to the absent king and report on important events in the capital city, Mari, including happenings and thoughts related to religion. All the letters demonstrate a remarkably independent activity on the part of the women in relation to offering sacrifices, receiving oracles, and other cultic measures and suggestions. They contribute nothing to our question about private cults since they speak only about the temple in the royal city. These women have been integrated into the national cult, even in matters of most intimate concern (for example, illness). Obviously, for the royal house, national cult and private cult converge.

In his 1975 study *Mein Gott*, Hermann Vorländer gathered voluminous ancient Near Eastern material referring to the practice of personal religion, making a major contribution to the recognition of the family and domestic cult. He asks: "Did women also have a personal god?" (p. 46). And he answers decisively: one must "draw the conclusion that women, too, were able to worship a (male or female) deity as a personal god. It is probable that in many cases this would have been identical to the personal god of her husband and his family" (p. 47). In this regard, Vorländer points to three texts. In one ancient Babylonian letter, the divine protector is called *ilu nasiru* ("protecting God"), and the author of the letter directs the blessing of this deity to the woman to whom he is writing: "May the God protecting you not be discontent" (pp. 20–21). An ancient Babylonian contract includes among the duties of a concubine that she "carry her [the wife's] chair . . . to the temple of her god" (p. 46). Occasionally, Mesopotamian seals used by women (women were at least sometimes active in business in the ancient Near East) include, after a personal name, "servant [fem.] of the god X." An example says, "Marat-Taribu, servant [fem.] of Sin (and) of Nergal" (p. 47). In other words, at least among the Mesopotamian cultures, a woman could maintain a personal relationship with a deity. This is documented in many more texts than those cited here. Some of these texts may refer to a domestic cult. In any event, the Mesopotamian woman had access to the cult not only by way of her husband. Familial religion was frequently directed toward the divine/demonic pair *sedu* and *lamassu*. *Lamassu* is a female deity; *sedu* a male godlike being. It is doubtful, though possible, that the two were always addressed together as a pair. Vorländer thinks the stereotypical formulation within the prayers is misleading. The frequent terms "my god" and "my goddess" may merely indicate where the man or woman saying the prayer would insert the name of the deity to whom he or she wanted to appeal. There are texts, however, which call upon only one of the partners of a divine pair.

Finally, in her 1974 book *Die alten Ägypter* (4th ed., 1987), Emma Brunner-Traut seeks to describe everyday life in the kingdom of the pharaohs using unofficial documents—from clay shards to wall graffiti, from satire to the notes of school children. In the process she occasionally touches cultic practices related to women and the household. Magic, rites, and prayers especially surround the pregnant woman, the process of birth in the maternity arbor, and the new mother (pp. 50–67). The woman was the main cultic participant in these situations, although later, after her purification, she resumed her place in the regular household ceremonies (see p. 64). Like Mesopotamian conjuring, Egyptian healing ceremonies took place in the private dwelling or locality of the patient (p. 52); the death cult, at least for well-off Egyptians, was practiced in the tomb of the individuals involved. This information does not exhaust the reports of domestic cultic ceremonies in the ancient Near East, but comprehensive detailed investigations are lacking.

Archaeological discoveries can, of course, expand and illuminate the written traditions. The number of excavated figures of gods and goddesses has now reached the thousands. As a rule, these sculptures are 10 to 20 centimeters high. They have been found in tombs, in and around temples, but above all in dwellings (U. Winter, 128). The Israelite city of Mizpah, 13 kilometers north of Jerusalem, offers a striking example. American archaeologists found there more than ninety figurines, distributed throughout the entire city. Excavators at Mizpah and other sites also discovered small cultic objects such as altars, incense stands, and offering tables. These cultic objects also point to a domestic form of divine worship. Among the figurines, goddesses far outnumber the male gods. Many researchers are inclined to see these as household idols. The preference for female deities could then indirectly indicate a leading role for women in family worship. Women were particularly responsible for fertility and offspring and thus became the appropriate mediators of the goddess and primal mother, the giver of all life. Especially interesting for us is the fact that so many of these goddess figurines show up in Israelite cities, even of the royal period. Thus, the domestic cult survived from the earliest beginnings to the time of the centralized government; only later, as a consequence of the new organization of Israel after the royal era, did it come into conflict with an exclusive official faith in Yahweh.

Our preliminary result is this: The Israelite woman presumably played a prominent role in domestic worship through all the many changes in social structure and official religion. The after-effects of her responsibility for the family's faith can be found even today in the Judeo-Christian tradition. Religious education of children is still almost exclusively left to mothers, even though the theme of fertility has receded in today's marriages and has been replaced by other interests. Even in our desacralized world, women often maintain a connection to spiritual or mythic powers and to a community of faith, while men have frequently distanced themselves from any form of religious faith or from the church (for Germans, often because of the church tax).

6 | The God of the Fathers

Having investigated in the preceding chapter the (female) internal aspects of Israel's oldest familial religion, we now turn to its (presumably male) external dimensions. Here we enter the prehistorical era that preceded the tribal organization of Israel. Our tacit assumption is that the religious ideas of that earlier period continued their influence during the historical era. So, what were the dominant ideas about God among the pre- or proto-Israelites, before the time when it became possible for Deborah to call the separate groups to battle in the name of the tribal deity Yahweh? What was the gender of the deity in that early period? How was that early Hebraic society structured? Obviously we cannot expect to find written sources clearly datable to the epoch prior to 1200 B.C.E. The Old Testament retains some memory of pre-Mosaic conditions, primarily in the ancestral narratives and in isolated songs and proverbs, but direct witnesses are no longer available. The oldest passages in the Old Testament have been transformed through their use by later writers and adapted to newer situations. Thus, more than ever, we are dependent upon cautious backward extrapolations.

One such extrapolation was made in 1929 by Albrecht Alt, who concluded that the form of religion in the pre-Israelite ancestral period was clearly distinguishable from later Yahwistic faith. Abraham, Isaac, and Jacob had not yet met the God Yahweh; in the words of Josh 24:2, they "lived beyond the Euphrates and served other gods." Exod 6:2–3 correctly maintains: "I am [Yahweh]. I appeared to Abraham, Isaac, and Jacob as God Almighty [El Shaddai], but by my name '[Yahweh]' I did not make myself known to them." Consequently, Exod 3:14 marks the beginning of Yahwistic faith with the revelation of the name Yahweh to Moses on Mt. Sinai. But what came before that? Whom did the patriarchal groups worship in matters other than fertility and offspring? Albrecht Alt's interpretation of the old narratives brings to light ancient ideas and ancient memories (as in Thomas Mann's *Joseph and His Brothers*). Moreover, Alt draws analogies from Israel's environment, primarily from Nabatean and Palmyrene inscriptions that derive from similar social structures and sometimes contain formulations similar to the ancestral narratives of the Old Testament. Alt came to the conclusion that in the early seminomadic, patriarchal period, each independent Hebrew clan had its own patron deity. This deity had once revealed itself to the patriarch of the group and was thereafter worshiped under the name "the God of X (the patriarch)," for example, "the God of Abraham." Other common titles, also showing the association of the deity with the tribal patriarch, are "the Fear of Isaac," "the Shield of Abraham," and "the Mighty One of Jacob." In other words, the familial deity was closely, if not exclusively, connected to the head of the family and through him to the entire clan that worshiped that deity. Moreover, the forceful names Fear, Shield, and Mighty One indicate that the God of the father assumed primarily external protective functions, accompanying and caring for the nomadic clan.

As one might expect, Albrecht Alt's hypothetical reconstruction of the religion of the fathers has not gone without criticism. Unanimity among exegetical specialists is hardly to be expected, especially for that twilight period of pre-Israelite history. Insofar as those who disagree do not regard the whole patriarchal religion of the ancestral narratives as historically unfounded later speculations, their counterproposals or additions to Alt's thesis lie in the following areas.

1. Following the old pan-Babylonian school, some scholars assert that the first fathers of Israel, stemming from a Chaldean homeland (Gen 11:28, 31), would have worshiped Sin, the Sumerian moon god. They note that the cities of Ur in southern Mesopotamia and Haran on the middle Euphrates were specially favored cultic sites of this deity (who was also worshiped in Babylon). Feminist interpretation of the Old Testament has given

new importance to this thesis, because the worship of the moon
has been seen by many female scholars of religion as belonging
originally to women and as a sign of matriarchy. "The threefold
moon is a symbol of the threefold goddess of matriarchy in its
highest stage of development" (H. Göttner-Abendroth, 5). There
is evidence for a moon cult in the cities of Ur and Haran. Moreover, the names of certain relatives of Abraham—Terah (ibex?)
and Laban (the "white one")—may point to worship of the moon.
Nevertheless, it remains doubtful that the religion of the pre-
Israelite seminomads can be connected to the moon cult. The Old
Testament lacks any clear references to such a thing, and placing
Abraham's origins in Ur may well be more later projection than
historical fact. In addition, the worship of the moon in northern
and middle Mesopotamia was in all probability an urban affair,
hardly a characteristic of nomadic religions. Any attempt to identify the type of religion among the Hebrew ancestors must always
take into consideration the social structure connected with that
religion.

   2. The Old Testament often speaks of the patriarchs' beliefs in
various El-deities. The reader encounters an El-Bethel, that is,
the god El from Bethel (Gen 31:13; 35:7); an El-'Olam from
Beer-sheba (Gen 21:33); an El-Roi, that is, an El who sees me (?)
(Gen 16:13); an El-Elyon, a god most high (Gen 14:18–20, and
often); an El-Shaddai, an El of the mountains (?) (Gen 17:1); and
an El-berith (or Baal-berith) from Shechem, that is, an El of the
covenant (Judg 9:4, 46). No matter how fully these titles, in their
present biblical contexts, have been adopted by Yahwistic faith,
they represent a Canaanite El-religion that was distinct from
Yahwism, even though it may often have been directly identified
with Yahweh; this Canaanite religion was associated with many
local sanctuaries and deities. A careful comparison with the Ugaritic myths confirms the impression that the El-religion was widespread in the ancient Near East, especially in Syria and Canaan,
and that its manifestations in the Old Testament (that is, in the
region of the later Israelite tribes) represent local adaptations of
this religion honoring the queen of heaven and the creator god.
In order to assert that the ancient Hebraic ancestors of Israel were
originally connected with this El-religion, one would need to

demonstrate that they came out of the Canaanite urban proletariat. Up to now, such proof has been lacking. Therefore, it seems virtually impossible to postulate such a religion among the migrating nomadic groups. Worship of the high god seems to be a typically urban religious form, as already understood by Alt in the basic essay mentioned earlier. For Alt, El-deities were tied to the established sanctuaries of settled communities.

3. A few American scholars have assumed that the patriarchs never worshiped any other god than Yahweh. Their view comes close to the orthodox Jewish interpretation that begins with the unity and immutability of God's revelation. J. Philip Hyatt, for example, assumes Yahweh was one of the ancient patriarchal deities who finally prevailed (pp. 78–81). And Frank Cross comes to the conclusion that the name Yahweh is finally nothing but an abbreviated El-name. Its fuller form would be: *El du yahwi (saba'ot)*, or "El creates (the hosts of heaven)." However, this interpretation of the patriarchal religion contradicts the clear witness of the Old Testament itself regarding the break between the religion of the fathers and the Mosaic faith.

Traditionally, as we see, the discussion of patriarchal religion has been concerned only with the tension between envisioning God as El or Yahweh. In view of the social realities, one can conclude, on the basis of the clear witness of the Old Testament, that the religion of the pre-Israelite period was based in the family or clan. One cannot, of course, exclude the possibility of occasional contact between the nomadic small-animal herdsmen of the ancient Near East and the land-based religion of the settled Canaanites, which may have included participation by the nomads in the worship of El-deities at pilgrimage sites and local temples. Alt's thesis of a clan religion is supported by evidence from Israel's neighboring peoples and cultures (see especially H. Vorländer) and from anthropological and sociological observations and suggestions. There has always been and always will be a small-group cult, that is, a particular religion of the smallest social group; its concerns are the elemental needs of primary human groups and of the individuals within those groups. Rites of passage observing transitions from one stage of life to another, healing the sick, and private celebrations have always been a matter for small or primary groups. Even today, baptism, confirmation, marriage, burial, and similar cultic events are of great importance for the family and the extended clan. Even where religion is controlled by an established church, these events seek and find their own specific rites, practices, and modes of belief. In the midst of all this, today or thousands of years ago, one finds a deity (god or goddess) who provides private protection and blessing—at this level, without concern for the well-being or the troubles of the "other" or the state.

But this whole debate about the proto-Israelite ancestral religion has now become sidetracked. No matter how diverse one thinks the faith of the pre-Mosaic era, male scholars have generally assumed a patriarchally structured, seminomadic or urban Hebrew population. From there, they suggest or simply take for granted that the God of the pre-Mosaic period must also have been male (see W. Thiel). Their supporting arguments are sociological. Given the notions of that day, how could the protection of the nomadic group be ascribed to other than a male deity? Moreover, comparable data from Arabic, African, and American seminomadic or nomadic societies indicate that such nonsettled ways of life regularly lead to patriarchal structures in both society and religion. Opposing this view, feminist scholars (male and female) have accepted as axiomatic that pre-Mosaic Israel fostered a matriarchal social and religious order (see H. Göttner-Abendroth; G. Weiler; C. Mulack; R. von Ranke-Graves). We need to examine relevant texts to bring some clarity to this issue.

We cannot expect the Old Testament to provide theoretical statements or careful descriptions of the nature and function of the ancestral gods. To find answers to our questions, we will have to examine critically texts that preserve echoes from the early period. We begin with the following texts, which reflect a patriarchal clan religion and social order.

The covenant between Jacob and Laban (Gen 31:43–54) provides important evidence for the thesis of Albrecht Alt. The text has been frequently reworked, but its essential content is easily discernible. Two competing clans, related by marriage, seek to secure their territory and other interests over against each other through an agreement between their leaders. Laban is particularly concerned with the protection of his two daughters, who have been given in marriage to Jacob (see vv. 43, 50). The agreement can be guaranteed only by *both* clan deities, the God of Abraham and the God of Nahor (v. 53). A later redactional addition—"the God of their father" (v. 53)—attempts to blur the apparent polytheism of the ancestors. Some Hebrew manuscripts and the Greek Septuagint do not yet contain this addition. Thus, as required in a public legal controversy, each clan chief calls upon his respective deity, sealing the agreement with an oath and a ritual sacrifice. They erect a stone monument, certainly meant as a dwelling place and observation post for the deities. Mizpah means, after all, "watchtower." In the explanation offered by v. 49 (may the deity "watch between you and me, when we are absent one from the other"), the name "Yahweh" is a secondary addition. The actors in this story, standing under the protection and guaranty of the clan deities, are the heads of the two families: Laban and Jacob. The two women, whose destiny is also at stake, have no legal status; and the protective household god or goddess remains hidden under the saddle on Rachel's camel. The loss of his teraphim has no effect on Laban's ability to do business. The clan deity called upon here is almost certainly male. At any rate, all levels of the tradition unanimously use the masculine grammatical gender for the deities of the two fathers. The same can be said of the common grammatical usage of the word *elohim* ("god," "deity"). The three applicable forms of the general term for god (*el, elo'ah, elohim*), which, taken together, occur some 2,600 times in the Old Testament, are used only a very few times for female deities—for example, in 1 Kgs 11:5. Such a reading is impossible in our story, and none of the recognizable sources can be said to have been retouched by patriarchal hands. Briefly stated, in this first story about the early ancestral deity, we find a typical example of the male religion of that era, operating in the realm of external relations among the clans. The preceding story of the theft of the teraphim, which is responsible internally for blessing the household, shows clearly the bifurcation of the ancient clan religion.

Gen 28:10–22 contains God's great epiphany to Jacob near Bethel. It has been deemed the key event of a new family religion. In that reading, the ancestor is on his way to visit relatives in Mesopotamia and makes a contract with a deity that appears to him. "If God will be with me, and will keep me in this way that I go, and will give me bread to eat and clothing to wear, so that I come again to my father's house in peace, then Yahweh shall be my God" (Gen 28:20–21). A literal translation shows immediately that the name Yahweh is a later addition: "If God (Elohim) will be with me . . . then Yahweh shall be my God." If we take the original text as the expression of familial religion (and at the very least it is accurately patterned after the clan situation), then some of the primary expectations of a clan deity become quite clear. The whole story is about personal protection, the presence and accompaniment of the divine being, especially for the head of the family. The protective relationship is mediated through him to all his dependents. In the case of Jacob this even includes those not yet born, just as in some contemporary legal or insurance contracts. The Jacob story concerns itself concretely with nourishment, clothing, and defense against those enemies and dangers encountered in travel—in other words, not with the kind of blessing that would guarantee the fertility of an agricultural existence. We could say that the relationship with a protective clan deity is the primary content of the male-oriented public familial cult. The many promises of offspring and of becoming a great nation to the ancestors in the book of Genesis may appear to contradict this observation, but they do not belong to the original form of the patriarchal narratives. They presume the existence of a people, "Israel," that confirms its own existence through these promises. The promise of offspring may have been made originally to the woman (see Judges 13; 1 Samuel 1). On the other hand, the ceremony described in Exod 21:6, in which a man held in temporary slavery was brought before the familial deity at the door of the house and obligated to lifelong servitude, is not, as it may seem, an "internal" household matter. It is actually a public and legal act for which the husband alone is responsible, since only he can represent the family in external affairs. That does not, however, exclude the wife's access to and responsibility for the images of the household god or goddess in the course of her daily duties.

The story of Micah and his idol mentioned earlier (Judges 17) is like a later echo of the original clan religion. Well-to-do people,

especially large landowners, not only possessed a small statue of
the deity in a niche next to the door but could afford their own
domestic chapel and perhaps even a house chaplain. The beginning of the story tells how such a private shrine might have origi-
nated; the story serves, no doubt, to discredit the idol, which
would shortly be forcibly abducted by the tribe of Dan.

> There was a man in the hill country of Ephraim whose name was Mi-
> cah. He said to his mother, "The eleven hundred pieces of silver that
> were taken from you, about which you uttered a curse, and even spoke
> it in my hearing,—that silver is in my possession; I took it; but now I
> will return it to you." And his mother said, "May my son be blessed by
> Yahweh!" Then he returned the eleven hundred pieces of silver to his
> mother; and his mother said, "I consecrate the silver to Yahweh from
> my hand for my son, to make an idol of cast metal." So when he re-
> turned the money to his mother, his mother took two hundred pieces
> of silver, and gave it to the silversmith, who made it into an idol of
> cast metal; and it was in the house of Micah. This man Micah had a
> shrine, and he made an ephod and teraphim, and installed one of his
> sons, who became his priest. (Judg 17:1–5)

This narrative shows us something of the internal family life
of a patriarchal landowner during the premonarchial period. To
be sure, the head of the family is not mentioned. Perhaps the son
had taken the place of a deceased father. But what actually happens in this estate "in the hill country of Ephraim" (Judg 17:1)?
Do Micah and his mother have an idol made for their house (perhaps a wooden figure covered with precious metal)? Do they obtain an ephod (perhaps a cultic mask or an oracle bag) and teraphim for an already existing chapel? Is a new familial cult
established here? Why does the mother regularly speak of Yahweh when she is obviously having an image made of another deity? Or are the various cultic objects, made of the stolen and restored silver, meant to represent Yahweh himself? How does the
narrator view the mother's relation to this new domestic cult, apparently established as an act of propitiation? And what about her
relation to the son, who had embezzled or misappropriated this
huge sum from his mother's fortune and then, in repentance, returned it in order to ward off the curse?

Let us assume that the original form of this brief story was not a propaganda legend against the later sanctuary at Dan, which was equipped with the stolen furnishings of Micah's domestic chapel. Let us assume the story reflects the religious realities of Israel's early period. Then it is worth noting that a family shrine is either established or extended through an act of expiation apparently meant to remove the force of a curse already spoken. Similar motives have played a role in Christian history in the building of many churches and cloisters. But what about the distribution of gender roles in Judges 17? Micah's mother apparently lives as a rich widow with her equally well-to-do son, who handles money quite loosely. She may well be the mistress of the estate. At any rate, she has a large reserve of pure silver. Her son pilfers the treasure, and she pronounces a terrible curse on the unknown thief. Such curses were taken very seriously at that time, as they still are in preindustrial tribal societies. The son admits he is the thief; the mother seeks to call back or neutralize the curse and suggests the building of a family chapel. In that patriarchal society, the one responsible for carrying out the construction is the son (perhaps also because he, as the wrongdoer, is the one who must make atonement). The mother apparently has nothing officially to do with the cultic image and the oracular instruments of the deity, who watches over the family's external possessions. But it is her idea and her money, and she determines what needs to happen. Though they have different positions, the two leading figures of an extended family, a woman and a man (in this case, a mother and her son), bear common responsibility for the family cult. This is, then, a very different picture from the one in Genesis 28. Yet, it shares with the two Jacob stories previously mentioned the idea that the family deity is represented in external affairs only by the man; for in Judges 17–18, it is finally Micah who is seen as the owner of the chapel and the idol.

The external, patriarchal face of the ancestral religion shows up again in a much later section of the Hebrew Bible. The Rechabites, known as particularly zealous followers of Yahweh (see 2 Kgs 10:15–17), remained faithful to bedouin ideals up to the time of Jeremiah and the Babylonian conquest. As refugees in the capital city of Jerusalem, they are still committed to the ancestral nomadic life, live in tents, and steadfastly refuse to partake in the joys or activities of the settled areas. Even though it is not expressly stated, their position has a religious basis, or at least religious consequences. Here we see again the combination of patrilinear clan structure and patriarchal decision-making in public affairs. The men of the clan deal with the prophet, set the norms of behavior for all members of the clan (or follow the norms of their ancestor Jehonadab), and maintain these norms even in the urban setting. In external matters, the women and children are bound to these forms of the common life. The text says nothing about domestic or internal life in this carefully demarcated environment. Yahweh is the male protecting deity of this family, as he presumably is in all of the previously mentioned texts. However, the appearance of other deity pairs (Tarpis and Anaris, Lamassu and Sedu) permits us to assume that, at least in theory, the clan could also have had female protecting deities. If the name "Shamgar son of Anath" (Judg 3:31; 5:6) refers to the Canaanite goddess Anath (about which there can be little doubt), we would have at least one reference to a female protecting family deity in Israelite tradition. But the worship of a household goddess, even by the head of the family, does not automatically point to a matriarchal familial structure.

We would like to know much more about the role of the sexes in the familial religion of early Israel. Our texts point primarily to the external patriarchal structure of the domestic religious life. Only seldom do we catch a glimpse of the religious responsibility and cultic activity of the woman of the house. However, from everything we know about tribal societies, female and male religiosity existed at the family level with a certain polarity and balance. Thus, we dare not let ourselves be misled by the so apparently one-sided masculine religious world of Israel's ancestors.

We must still turn briefly to another source to help us understand the clan religion of premonarchic Israel. It confirms for us the picture of a familial cult whose external affairs are determined by men. That source is the many personal names handed down to us in the Hebrew Bible. They offer uncontaminated data about the faith and hope of the name-givers. Since the social setting of names and naming is primarily the small circle of the primary group, personal names, as a rule, reflect the conditions and relationships of that family group. In general, ancient peoples were very religious. They often gave their children names that had the character of prayer or praise. Daughters were not always simply called "Little Bee" (Deborah) or "Date Palm" (Tamar), sons were certainly not always "Fool" (Nabal) or "Red" (Edom). Instead, people included in the names words of thanks, praise, and petition to God. The deity might be identified by its own name or with generic designations. These theophoric names consist either of a nominative sentence or expression or of a complete or abbreviated sentence with an active verb. Grammatically, such a sentence makes a statement about the deity. Thus, as far as the bearer of the name goes, it is gender neutral. "God has heard" (Ishmael, Elishama, or Shemaiah) could theoretically be the name for either a boy or a girl. In practice, however, theophoric personal names are found predominantly among men. This indicates that the relationship to the protecting familial deity was carried in a legal or public sense by the clan's male line. Furthermore, name-giving functioned according to similar rules and patterns among all the Semitic cultures surrounding Israel. Many researchers have therefore become frustrated, believing they can, at best, derive information from Semitic personal names only about a nonspecific cultural religiosity, not about Yahwism in particular. After all, every Semitic culture ascribes to a variety of deities the same qualities, such as "lord," "light," "helper," and so on, and the same activities, such as "hearing," "saving," "protecting," "leading," and so on. But for our purposes, this is important data, showing that name-giving takes place in the bosom of the family, without reference to larger issues of politics or theology. The names are unabashedly oriented toward the needs of the small group and the intimate common life of a limited number of people. That is why they are so similar among the different cultures and religious groups. Whether they include the name of a "private" deity or a high official god, all names speak, in principal, about the protective deity with whom the extended family maintains solidarity. Rainer Albertz aptly demonstrated this in his book *Persönliche Frömmigkeit und offizielle Religion*. His study deepened and extended the pioneering work of Hermann Vorländer. So far, we have no comprehensive study of gender-specific relationships to the deity on the basis of Semitic personal names (see J. J. Stamm). Let us return to the question of family religion. Albertz established that the great themes of Israelite theology—exodus, election, revelation at Sinai, Davidic monarchy, and so on—are completely absent from Israel's name-giving. Instead, the names refer to familial experiences, to everyday tests and recognitions of faith, and to the small family cult, which was always practiced in the context of the small group, never in one's own private chamber. We can divide the personal names roughly into two major groups: First, those names that express an existing relationship of protection, trust, or relatedness to the clan deity, like "God is father" (Abiel; compare also Abijah, Abimelech, Abibaal) or "God is brother" (Ahiel; compare also Ahijah, Ahimelech). In a more or less metaphorical or symbolic sense, the protecting deity is addressed as a male relative. Names with female theophoric elements, of the type "God is mother," or "aunt," or "sister," are unknown in the Old Testament. They seem to have been uncommon in the ancient Near Eastern Semitic cultures as well, although the confessional statement "God is father and mother" was, in fact, part of the prayer terminology among Israel's neighbors. Other expressions belonging to the group of relational names include "God is the protecting deity" (Eliel; compare also Eliab, Eliam, Elijah, Elimelech) or "God is wholeness" (Shelumiel; compare also Shelemiah, Abishalom), "God is help" (Eliezer; compare also Joezer, Ahiezer), and "God is deliverance" (Elishua; compare also Joshua, Abishua, Malchishua). Although it cannot be established in every case, the protecting deity in these names should generally be regarded as male.

The other large group of personal names describes God's desired or experienced intervention in favor of the name-bearer and his or her group. Many different verbs appear that indicate a turning toward humanity—saving, healing, helping, or securing justice. Some examples: Ishmael or Samuel express the confession "God has heard" or the wish "May God hear." Correspondingly, Jerahmeel presumably means either "God has had mercy" or "May God have mercy." We can translate Zechariah with "Yahweh has thought"; Pelatiah with "Yahweh has saved"; Pedahzur with "The god Zur has ransomed"; Gealjahu with "Yahweh has redeemed"; Rephael with "God has healed"; Gamaliel with "God has shown good"; Jehoshaphat with "Yahweh has done justice"; and so on. Female deities are not found among these names either. The appearance of the goddess Anath in the genealogy of the judge Shamgar (Judg 3:31; 5:6) remains unique. However, place names do sometimes make reference to goddesses—for example, Ashtaroth (1 Chr 6:71) refers to the goddess Astarte.

We have come, historically and socially, to a conclusion—or, better, to a beginning—for Israel's traditions of faith. For millennia, faith and worship had been a matter of the smallest human communities, before the construction of regional and national temples and theologies. The elemental human desire for a protecting deity stands at the beginning of all religions, prior to and alongside the need for fertility and blessing. This has continued into the present, through all social and economic change. From earliest times the men of the family assumed the protective functions. Therefore, the cult of the protecting deity is dominated by men. Concern for fertility and household harmony seems to have come into the foreground only in agricultural societies (E. Badinter). At that time, the role of women in the domestic cult was strengthened. But nowhere in the ancient Near East was there a matriarchal religion in the political forefront. Instead, the oldest clans—consisting of female gatherers or agricultural workers and male hunters or herdsmen—had a bipolar religious and gender structure in which the accent shifted back and forth (see S. de Beauvoir; E. Badinter). Externally, these clans always exhibited male leadership and male protection.

At this point, we must register two reservations for the contemporary discussion. First, we no longer live in economically self-sufficient family groups. Industrial society has turned human beings into individuals who may continue to live, pro forma, under one roof. Consequently, the patriarchal or matriarchal images of God derived from old clan structures are no longer usable in our time. Their place in our most personal and private beliefs must be taken by an understanding of God that is derived from and compatible with a democratic society.

Second, we need to understand that major religions are neces-

sary, but secondary, constructions. Of course, theology must reflect the global and universal relationships of human beings. More
than ever, we need a truly comprehensive understanding of the
world and God, one that effectively overcomes our chauvinisms
and particular interests. Nevertheless, the basic foundation of our
personal piety, that is, of our primary groups and the individuals
who live in them, dare not be overlooked; the interests of small
social organisms dare not be trampled and overrun. A church that
places at the center of its consciousness and activity a worship
service abstracted from everyday life and oriented only toward
large groups—a church that neglects or despises its occasional
pastoral acts, pastoral care, small groups, organizations, and similar activities—has misconstrued its task. At the lower levels of the
church's practical work, in which people come into direct contact
with one another, one meets predominantly women. In the administrative superstructure, however, the number of men remains
disproportionally large. Paying attention to the church's small
group structure will also mean, de facto, recognizing the work
and responsibility of women in the church.

7 | *The Patriarchal God*

So far, we have moved through the major phases of Israel's religious history, proceeding from the youngest to the oldest levels of Old Testament tradition, and have discovered very different socially and historically determined images of God. Particularly in regard to sexuality and fertility, the Bible alludes to discordant theological conceptions, which to some degree continue up to this day. This comes as no surprise if we analyze the sources of our own faith in addition to the biblical witness. But such work will not be content with an analysis and comparison of images of God from Israel's past. We need a meaningful and analytical comparison of the old witnesses to our own contemporary experiences.

This raises an immediate and fundamental problem. The Bible cannot provide us with a timeless and universally binding image of God. The Old Testament, at least, lacks even the most basic rudiments of a unified and consistent doctrine of God that is clearly formulated and that spans the generations. Instead, we encounter several time-conditioned statements of faith that can in no way simply be repeated in our own situation. But this dilemma only seems to be insoluble. In fact, it reflects the task of theology in every generation, namely, to dare independent and timely statements about God in dialogue with the witness of the past. Theology dare not hide behind our ancestors; it must relate to the situation of the present world and the contemporary search for God. Just as surely as the living God of the biblical witness is still at work today, the images of God that we sketch in response to that work must differ from those of the Bible. Seen in that persepective, the variety of theological traditions in the Bible itself does not hinder but rather provides a license for our search for a proper contemporary confession of God. This license does not open the door to limitless caprice but provides room for a responsible theological task, to be undertaken in the name of God and all humanity.

We can sketch the special problem that concerns us here as follows. For long periods, the Old Testament history of faith gave both sexes, of various social classes, room for their particular expressions of faith. To be sure, from the beginning, patriarchal structures dominated in Israel and in the pre-Israelite clans. But within the male-oriented external structure, women had their own areas of domestic religious life for which they remained responsible. For a long time, Israel, too, worshiped both god and goddess. The concentration of cult and faith on the one God Yahweh began only in the era of the Babylonian exile; the final result of this was the catastrophic exclusion of or discrimination against women. Feminist theologians regularly and rightly put their finger on this sore point. The overwhelming majority of male Jewish and Christian theologians and church leaders have made arrogant and sexist decisions and judgments at the expense of women. They did this in the name of that unique and exclusive God who, despite lip service to his otherness, was viewed as a male. This fact is indisputable, and thus should not be suppressed, glossed over, or endlessly debated. From the prohibition of "mixed marriages" in late Old Testament texts to the degradation of women by many of the church fathers, to the persecution of witches at the beginning of the modern era, and to the exclusion of women from the priestly office and other areas of church leadership, there has been a straight line of male admiration of self and contempt for women in the Judeo-Christian tradition. Under the umbrella of religious ideas and values, women have been treated unjustly in church and society a million times over. We can no longer overlook this reality in our search for an appropriate contemporary image of God. But how did Israel come to this fatal limitation of their notion of God? What were the reasons for excluding women and the goddess from the cultic activity of the Old Testament people of God? If we now want to remove this millennia-old injustice, we must, insofar as possible, shed light on its causes. A false diagnosis can lead only to malpractice and the failure to employ the necessary measures toward radical reform.

It appears that the sexist constriction of Israel's image of God was not originally a malicious and "necrophilic" plan of criminal male minds, but rather the unplanned long-term consequence of the decision, for quite unrelated reasons, to worship the "only God" Yahweh. If that is true, we would need to examine first the monotheistic concentration of Israel's faith in God and only secondarily the emergence of a sexist notion of male superiority and the corresponding devaluation of the female in the context of theology and the community of faith.

The most important Old Testament writings from the sixth century B.C.E.—Second Isaiah, Jeremiah, Ezekiel, the deuteronomistic history (Deuteronomy 1 through 2 Kings 25)—give no evidence that the Israelite theologians of that period opted primarily for a male deity and against a female one. The only possible exception is Jer 44:15–19, discussed in chapter 1. Otherwise, the primary decision is for *one* God, Yahweh, who had been known in Israel since the tribal era, and against the *other* gods and goddesses of Israel's environment. "Hear, O Israel: Yahweh is our God, Yahweh alone. You shall love Yahweh your God with all your heart, and with all your soul, and with all your might" (Deut 6:4–5). That has been and still is the core of exilic or postexilic Jewish faith. Precisely, it does not say that Yahweh is a *male* God, but that Yahweh is the *only* God (as far as Israel is concerned). Yahweh's sexuality is not a theological problem for the Deuteronomists. Yahweh is by nature incomparable and therefore cannot be pictured (Deuteronomy 4). Nothing in this world can represent the divine nature pictorially. "He" is neither "man" nor "woman" (Deut 4:16). In those days, the gender contradiction now apparent to us in such a sentence went unnoticed. Because of this view of God, the decalogue enjoins the double prohibition: You shall have no other gods before me; and You shall not make for yourself an idol (Deut 5:6–10). And everywhere the fundamental chapters of deuteronomistic theology press the command to love and worship Yahweh. Faith in the only God requires full and exclusive devotion to him. Though Yahweh is quite naturally named in masculine forms, we observe nevertheless no conscious sexist overtones or undertones in the deuteronomistic admonitions.

It is true that the devotees of Yahweh, in their conflict with what the sixth-century B.C.E. theologians regarded as idol worshipers, rejected Canaanite fertility religion and eventually also a foreign queen (Jezebel) who tempted them to apostasy. But none of this was done in the name of a principled preference for maleness in religious affairs (see 1 Kings 18). On the contrary, in the polemics between the circles faithful to Yahweh and the people subject to temptation, Israel is often termed the wife or bride of Yahweh (see Ezekiel 16; 23). Thus, the female gender in itself is thoroughly pleasing to God and worthy of theological usage. God not only holds it in high regard, he ascribes to it incredibly erotic characteristics: "For Yahweh delights in you and your land shall be married. For as a young man marries a young woman, so shall your builder marry you, and as the bridegroom rejoices over the bride, so shall your God rejoice over you" (Isa 62:4–5; compare Ezekiel 16). Given this background, the "woman" Israel's apostasy from Yahweh is seen as "playing the whore" with the male gods of Canaan. If the point were male sexism, one would expect instead a picture of the "son" Israel yielding to Canaanite goddesses. But in the Bible's sexual imagery it is always the beloved woman who is unfaithful to Yahweh. Listen to how Jeremiah addresses Israel: "How can you say, 'I am not defiled, I have not gone after the Baals'? Look at your way in the valley; know what you have done—restive young camel interlacing her tracks, a wild ass at home in the wilderness, in her heat sniffing the wind! Who can restrain her lust?" (Jer 2:23–24). "Can a girl forget her ornaments, or a bride her attire? Yet my people have forgotten me, days without number. How well you direct your course to seek lovers!" (Jer 2:32–33a). The image of the disloyal and faithless wives, Judah and Israel, permeates the third chapter of Jeremiah, forming a parallel to Ezekiel 23. This could be termed sexism only if those accusing Israel of unfaithfulness already meant to use the female personification itself to express their loathing and their charges of impurity. But the flow of the texts makes that interpretation impossible (see especially Ezekiel 16). In the view of the prophets (cf. Hos 4:4–11) and in their own self-understanding (see Ezra 9), the leading theologians are included within this female Israel.

The theological questions and doubts of the sixth century B.C.E. do not arise from the (unreflected) assignment of gender to Yahweh. It is rather Yahweh's presence, reliability, and power that have become debatable among the people. The political events—especially the conquest of Judah and the deportations of the leaders in 597 and 586 B.C.E., but also the continuing dependence upon and exploitation by the victors—destroyed the Israelites' confidence in God. "Yahweh has forsaken me, my LORD has forgotten me" (Isa 49:14), laments the destroyed city, seen as the female partner of the deity. "My way is hidden from Yahweh, and my right is disregarded by my God" (Isa 40:27), says a disappointed, "robbed and plundered" people (Isa 42:22). In the fifth/fourth century B.C.E., the congregation is still praying," Yahweh, our God, other lords besides you have ruled over us" (Isa 26:13). Is Israel's misery not necessarily proof of the national God's passivity or animosity? Has he become powerless? Is his time past? Has Yahweh revoked his promises to Abraham and David? Is he in his dwelling place, the temple of Jerusalem, or has he left the country? What was Israel's own role in bringing the catastrophe?

Theology provides the arena and the means for Israel's struggle for survival in the sixth century B.C.E.; thus, the image of God is primarily marked by an opposition to the "other gods." Yahweh stands with his people and vicariously for his people in a life-and-death battle against Marduk or Bel of Babylon. The second part of the book of Isaiah, Second Isaiah (Isaiah 40–55), is permeated by the polemic against the "idols" in which the issue is the proof of the superior power of the God of Israel, contrary to all appearances. Yahweh is the creator of the universe. He is the mythic restrainer of chaos. He has guided the destiny of the nations from the beginning. It was according to his will that Israel fell into dependence and shame, but they will now be brought out of it, restored and radiant. The old promises to his people are still in effect! They are actualized in a new exodus out of Babylonian captivity. For the God Yahweh is incomparably greater and stronger than the other gods. They shrink before him to mere idols—graven images who are imaginary, self-made, and dead (Isa

40:18–24; 44:6–20). Yahweh alone is "eternal," that is, unlimited by time. He is the Alpha and Omega (in the Greek tradition, from the initial and final letters of the Greek alphabet) or, in Hebrew, the first and the last (Isa 41:4; 44:6; 48:12). The theology of Second Isaiah reaches its climax in the sentence: "Besides me there is no god" (Isa 43:11; 44:6, 8; 45:6, 21). The other gods, especially those of Babylon, fall before Yahweh. They cannot stop the liberation of Israel (Isaiah 46).

The superiority of Yahweh in the battle for the existence and hegemony of his people is certainly an ancient element of Israel's faith. It derives from the tradition of the tribes of Yahweh and is found in many other Old Testament texts. But the idea reaches its full expression only when it is combined with exclusive monotheistic claims, and that happens in Second Isaiah.

One thing is clear in all of this: The God Yahweh, who was established as the sole deity of Israel from the sixth century B.C.E. on, was, in accord with the notions of the day, a male deity—insofar as sexual associations were made at all. But this monotheistic theology was concerned primarily with Israel's external protection and self-assertion, that is, with tasks for which men were responsible. Family life and fertility, the major areas of the female deities, in which women had responsibility, moved into the background during the lengthy political-religious crisis of a subjugated Israel. The whole community of faith sought its identity in the arena of external affairs, under male leadership. After the collapse of the monarchy and the royal bureaucracy, the male leadership elite consisted of clergy, for whom the theocratic ideal was a given, and the elders of the tribes, clans, and villages, who maintained certain patriarchal family traditions. We hear next to nothing about women in important public religious positions; when they are mentioned, it is in legends (for example, the Book of Esther), in which, despite all male political arrogance, female concerns always found refuge. The tone of the official religion was shaped absolutely by the theocratic interests of the priests and Levites. As the exclusive claims of the male Yahweh religion became more and more firmly established, traditions relating to women and the family could survive only by going underground and donning a mantle of orthodoxy. Included here are the female characteristics ascribed to Yahweh (as regularly emphasized by feminist theologians): Yahweh's "compassion," his "spirit" ("spirit" in Hebrew is grammatically feminine), his "wisdom," and his "love" (see P. Trible, *Rhetoric;* C. Mulack). The use of such sexually oriented terms demonstrates considerable openness to female realities even among the patriarchal theologians of this exilic and postexilic period.

The concentration on the one and only God Yahweh was not sexist in origin, but because of the patriarchal theocratic social structure, its effects inevitably were. Given the unconscious desires of the male minds that articulated and informed the notion of God, that notion inevitably succumbed to male interests, tasks, and anxieties, even though, from the outset, God was consciously understood to be transcendent (Deuteronomy 4; 1 Kgs 8:27; Ps 90:2). The exclusion of women from the cult and public life was to bear bitter fruit. Though God was essentially transcendent and beyond human sexuality, the image of God was in reality strongly tied to the male world—and since there was no female counterweight, this fact resulted increasingly in discrimination against women.

Ironically, the initial impetus toward discrimination apparently did not arise from a sexist plot on the part of the priests, but more as a theological accident. We already spoke of the unintended rise of a male Yahweh and the equally unintended identification of his partner people as bride or wife, an image required simply by the grammar. But with the acute consciousness of sin and guilt brought on by the catastrophe of 586 B.C.E., a very negative cast was given to Israel's behavior, a behavior described in female terms even though the male leaders were primarily responsible for it. "Whoredom" as a metaphor for religious and communal infidelity actually applied only to the males, who were the ones responsible for this development. But this reproach could easily be understood as a value judgment on women (modern psychologists would speak of the projection of one's own repressed guilt on another). The prophetic message in the books of Hosea, Jeremiah, and Ezekiel seems to demonstrate this development. When the only thing remaining is an image of God defined by men, female realities necessarily take on lesser value, both in heaven and on earth. Despite sincere self-criticism, male feelings of superiority become unconsciously identified with the image of God. A heightened consciousness of sin, negatively related to female behavior, brings with it an unexamined depreciation of womanhood that seems to come directly from God.

The basic features of the creation stories demonstrate this tendency. In the older form (Genesis 2), the man is created first, contrary to all biological reasoning and experience; the woman sees the light of day only by being brought forth from his body. It is scarcely difficult to recognize here a reflection of a male worldview, with its patriarchal hegemony and its higher valuation of male functions such as protection and work. The woman is a "helper," one who provides service to and is an extension of the first-created man. The "worldview is clearly androcentric" (Crüsemann, 57). The notion that the woman is the man's helper in the sense of being his "savior" is modern wishful thinking (see Terrien, 10–11). The hegemony of the "master of creation" is legitimized in the following chapter (Genesis 3) by the woman's susceptibility to sin, her disobedience to God. The younger report (Genesis 1) knows only a male-dominated humanity, divided into two sexes for the purpose of procreation and for reasons of purity (Gen 1:26–27). There is no syllable in either story describing a democratic equality of the sexes.

But once the "masculinizing" of the image of God took place, as a consequence of the monotheistic limitation to a single deity, and once the female was reputed to be unreliable in religious affairs, then powerful motifs from other traditions and life experiences easily attached themselves to the relation between the sexes. Looking back in history from today's perspective, it is impossible to postulate a direct causal connection between monotheism and a contemptuous view of women, but one can name factors that may have contributed to the latter development.

1. In every human society, the relation between the sexes demonstrates certain tensions, based in biology and function, that are exhibited in controversies about superiority. Is a woman better than a man? This and other such inherently contentious questions could be raised within a patriarchal system organized around the polarity of the sexes without any particular disadvantage to

one gender or the other. But as soon as such banter is raised to a
theological level and equipped with absolute value judgments, the
polar balance is disturbed. This seems already to have occurred in
the creation story or in its early interpretation. The resulting human and religious depreciation of women takes on additional
force in the Judeo-Christian and Muslim traditions, especially in
connection with the following two factors.

2. The social disintegration of the once self-sufficient economic unit of the extended family or clan always comes at the
expense of the weakest members of the social structure. When the
family can no longer earn an adequate income, women and children suffer first. That fact is already clear in many late Old Testament writings. According to Nehemiah 5, the Judean farmers
could no longer come up with the Persian taxes and levies. They
were compelled to take out loans or to sell children into servitude.
Wives, and especially concubines, may have suffered a similar
fate. The man was held to be the owner of the family's fortune.
He had to meet all external obligations. Consequently, he had to
pass on to his own family the pressures of producing more and
consuming less. The head of the family functioned as the foreman
of a small family business that was subject to the good or ill will of
the political and economic powers of the day. Trust and solidarity
among relatives disappeared. "Put no trust in a friend, have no
confidence in a loved one; guard the doors of your mouth from
her who lies in your embrace; for the son treats the father with
contempt, the daughter rises up against her mother, the daughter-
in-law against her mother-in-law; your enemies are members of
your own household" (Mic 7:5–6). Farmers lost their land, became dependent on wages, went into indentured service, and
ended up as a vagabond proletariat. Foreigners and collaborators
took possession of the land or bled dry the poor. "Working in
vain," that is, sowing and not reaping, or building houses only so
others could live in them, became the nightmare of the oppressed
populace (see Deut 28:29–34; Mic 6:15; Isa 62:8–9). These conditions hit the wife harder than the husband. Turning an entire population into a working proletariat (which is happening today
throughout the world at a terrifying rate) diminishes women more
than men. Above all, it is finally women who have to care for the

hungry children. Even in antiquity, men often shirked this responsibility; they withdrew, going underground or resorting to alcoholism. When the oppressor gains the upper hand, destroying the balance of power, male self-consciousness often passes its own feeling of inferiority on to the woman. Thus, the social denigration of women contributes to their religious disenfranchisement, and vice versa.

3. The priestly theology of purity had the greatest influence on the relation between the sexes. At least by the time of the reconstruction of the temple in 515 B.C.E., the priesthood in Jerusalem played a key role in the reorganization of the dispersed Judean population. To be sure, there were communities of the faithful far from the spiritual metropolis; to be sure, many congregations organized themselves in relative independence, holding services of word and prayer without blood sacrifices; to be sure, the Torah and those schooled in Torah were viewed with the highest respect; still, the temple and its personnel exerted a peculiar and unique influence that extended down to the last faithful Judean family.

But priestly theology was determined (to a degree that would dismay us) by ideas of holiness and purity, defined in opposition to that which was unholy and unclean. Described in the categories of modern physics, God, in that theology, would be like a ball of energy, a sphere of light, a center of power that would "explode" when brought into contact with other kinds of matter. And the consequences were catastrophic. In the vocabulary of ancient Israel, the clean and the holy absolutely exclude everything unclean and unholy. Two spheres of existence stand in complete and total opposition, and the woman was separated—based on ancient religious and magical regulations—from the holy not only by sharing the impurity common to all humanity, but especially through the impurity peculiar to the female. According to this view, in concentric circles of decreasing holiness, women are more distant from the center (the deity) than are laymen, who in turn are more distant than priests. Even further away than Israelite women are foreign men or women and those under the divine ban.

For the priests, the woman's greater distance from the divine was symbolized by menstruation (see Lev 15:19–30). Blood contains the power of life. No human being can come in contact with blood except the ordained priest carrying out his vicarious ministerial duties. All blood belongs to God alone. One might ask, therefore, whether the priests saw menstruating women as some kind of competition. Or did they merely want to hinder any uncontrollable and nonsalvific contact between the holy and any blood not shed by the hand of the priest? In any case, in their view, mere contact with a menstruating woman or with an object of her personal use led to temporary uncleanness. No modern fear of infection by disease organisms or contamination by radioactive or toxic material could have greater effect than their anxiety over touching something unclean or unholy.

Thus, monotheistic theology was joined by various prejudices and projections of the patriarchal elite, all working to the disadvantage of women. The product of this development was a God who was now patriarchal in the sexist sense of that term. Thus, the exclusion of women from the official cult and the official theology of Israel and early Judaism was not the result of a violent patriarchal seizure of power that suppressed and destroyed matriarchal structures. Rather, the suppression of the female came as a by-product of the growing concentration of male Israelite faith on a single jealous God. In the midst of great tribulation, the whole people had pledged itself to this one Yahweh in order to maintain its own identity. The one God became the primary and exclusive content of Israel's confession, a God distinct from the gods of the ruling powers. God's Torah and temple, and the signs of circumcision and sabbath that he instituted, became the concrete symbols of the one legitimate protecting deity. This God, in the theological perspective of the day, was completely transcendent and therefore without image or gender. Any representation of the deity was prohibited; it would bring God down to the human sphere, making him an instrument for human use. Not even an image-free theology and cult, however, could exclude the actual social conditions of the day, despite all attempts to the contrary by the theologians. The theology and society of the postexilic period were, as usual, determined by men. Thus, male ideas, dreams, and anxieties became concentrated in the image-free notion and worship of God. The prejudices, tensions, frustrations, and dominant urges exhibited by men, who were solely responsible for the cult, had to impact women negatively. This might have been effectively corrected had there been equal rights for women in the public sphere, but this was completely lacking. Nor was there was any longer a female deity available to guarantee the balance of the sexes within the patriarchy. Nevertheless, it is noteworthy that the *total* exclusion of women—as though they were representative of sin itself—was practiced only in a very few Jewish or Christian splinter groups. Moreover, because the patriarch represented the entire family, all its members were involved in faith in God. Occasional protest movements did provide women the same human rights as men (for example, the Jesus movement and several Hellenistic and gnostic groups; R. Ruether, 33ff.; E. Schüssler-Fiorenza). Conscious theological reflection seldom stooped to hatred of women or the open glorification of the male gender; instead, there were serious efforts to keep the image of God transsexual and neutral (though, as we have seen, these did not succeed).

None of this, however, is meant to excuse or minimize the sins of a masculinized theology. Indeed, the consequences of this patriarchal and sexist limitation of the divine image were and are catastrophic. What began as devotion to the one God and as an unconscious turning from or fending off female concerns provided theological support for men's ever-present basic mistrust of women; often it gave rise to an unalleviated and brutal denigration of women, including harassment and persecution. The so-called "dissolution of mixed marriages" (Ezra 10; Nehemiah 13) was only the first episode in a long history of Judeo-Christian hatred of women. It was periodically rekindled, reaching its gruesome high point, of course, in the witch trials of the Middle Ages. In addition to this acute depreciation, even torture, of women, the development of a one-sided male theology had equally serious consequences. The goddess disappeared from the thought and experience of early Jewish theology. Traces remained, of course, in the sabbath liturgy, in ideas about wisdom, and in cabalistic speculation (see C. Mulack)—and no doubt also in unwritten common beliefs. Mary and the female saints of the Roman Catholic Church provided refuge for religious expression that was specifically female. But official Judeo-Christian theology, which was completely a male construction (or nearly so), found little place for creation, procreation, birth, sexuality, and nature. At best, models that were developed in these areas were one-sidedly male, with corresponding norms of behavior that favored men and their privileged position.

The obvious question of whether discrimination against women was a necessary consequence of the decision for monotheism arises. In my opinion, the answer is no. Social conditions were responsible for the exclusion of the female. This can be confirmed by an all-too-brief examination of ancient polytheistic cultures and religions. To what extent was a pantheon of gods or the existence of goddesses a guarantee against the depreciation of women in cult and society? Women in the regions around Israel—Canaan, Mesopotamia, Egypt, and Asia Minor—were as a rule more highly valued and enjoyed more cultic responsibility than in post-exilic Judaism (see J. Ochshorn; I. Seibert). To some degree, laws concerning property, marriage, and family were demonstrably more liberal in these cultures than in the Old Testament. For example, according to the well-known legal code of the ancient Babylonian King Hammurapi, a woman could obtain a divorce, manage her own property, practice the "public" vocation of innkeeper, and so on. However, the fundamental patriarchal orders of society were in no way broken among the polytheistic cultures of the ancient Near East. Even where goddesses (hardly ever bothered, of course, by pregnancy and the raising of children), were extremely active participants in the controversies and ceremonies of the pantheon, the claim to male leadership in earthly public affairs went uncontested. It is therefore impossible to draw conclusions about a culture's social structure from its religious beliefs and divine myths. We simply lack the historical basis to claim that the cultures of the ancient Near East known to us from written sources were politically matriarchal or in transition from matriarchy to patriarchy. The overwhelming impression presented by countless legal and economic documents from Mesopotamia, dating back to the year 3000 B.C.E., is precisely the same as that found in the early levels of the Old Testament. Areas of responsibility were divided by gender and unalterably fixed by firm tradition. As I see it, the ancient world was marked by a more or less tolerable balance in the areas of responsibility and role assignments given to the sexes (cf. J. Ochshorn; J. M. Asher-Greve). To the man fell the outside work and the public representation of the family and the household. He was the "head of the household"— a designation that remained legally valid into our most recent history (see, for example, the German civil law code of 1896). Thus, a comparison of findings from the Old Testament with what we can learn about the place of women from ancient Near Eastern religions and legal systems leads to the overall impression that, prior to the Babylonian exile, the balance of the sexes in Israel corresponded to that found in neighboring ancient cultures. Things got worse for women in the postexilic period under the indirect influence of a consolidating monotheistic faith that was primarily male. Under the aegis of a single deity, who spoke only through male mouths, male prejudices developed with impunity and without inhibition or external control. Nevertheless, I find untenable an attempt to reconstruct a direct monocausal relationship between the rise of monotheism in Israel and the denigration of women. Ideas or images of God are never the sole causes of social change. If they were, then the history of slavery, for example, would have taken quite a different course. Still, the connection made in the Bible between women and sin shows how a particular theology under particular social and religious conditions can encourage discrimination against one group of human beings.

There are, no doubt, many reasons for the close association between women and evil in certain biblical traditions. For one thing, the different roles and functions of the sexes and the various interests and experiences of men and women have always quite naturally given rise to internal family conflicts. In our fondest dreams, we cannot envision people of mixed ages and sexes living together in total harmony and without tension, even in the fairest of societies. But the inevitable conflicts and anxieties, guilt feelings, and power claims can easily make people assign guilt to others, guilt which in turn can quickly become generalized: because some women *can* be, therefore all women *are* irritable and cranky (Prov 19:13; 21:9, 19; 25:24; 27:15–16). The opinionated

woman, who strongly asserts her role in household conflicts, becomes stereotyped in the biblical proverbs. In the face of her continual nagging and scolding (it is said), the husband wishes to
crawl into a corner in the attic. On the other hand, from the woman's point of view, a husband who forgets his public responsibilities and idles away his time with his drinking buddies is so far
removed from the demands of life that he can no longer make
realistic decisions. He is an incompetent and arrogant boob (1
Sam 25:25). In such a case, the woman must resolutely assume
responsibility for the family in order to avert catastrophe. In other
words, in the Old Testament we meet negative stereotypes of both
sexes. Both are derived from everyday experience and contain a
measure of truth. The division of labor can, even in "natural" social structures, typically lead to mistakes, chronic discontent, and
claims to dominance on the part of women as well as to a lord-
and-master arrogance, laziness, and alcoholism on the part of
men. Variations on the same theme include, for women (as viewed
by men), curiosity, gossip, vanity, and ostentation, and, for men
(as viewed by women), cowardice, caprice, narrow-mindedness,
and bragging. Native American men, for example, tell stories in
which the curiosity of women is the root of all the world's trouble.

In the second place, men have always experienced the female
sex as both attractive and dangerous at the same time. Sexual desire (even in the not-yet-sexualized society of the ancient world)
can carry away the young inexperienced male—though surely not
only him—plunging him into unholy entanglements (2 Samuel
11; 13; Proverbs 5; 7). From the Song of Songs we can infer that
things were basically the same for women, even though the Bible
does not provide further information from the female perspective. The male literature available to us portrays only the charm
and seductive arts of the woman, projecting the male's own desires
and failures on women. Occasionally, one finds a certain attempt
at objectivity (see Genesis 38; 2 Samuel 13), but in general the
woman's perspective is shortchanged. It is only the literature produced by women in the modern era and the change in consciousness standing behind it that allow a more balanced estimate of the
mutual blaming practiced by both men and women. One sees, in
fact, that in the give-and-take of the sexes, women can also associ-

ate men with evil. Sometimes, men are ascribed the entire blame for all disturbances in sexual relationships (see S. Firestone; S. Hite). As a counterbalance to the one-sided condemnations of women, even such indiscriminate judgments may have their place. Still, many women do strive, from their own perspective, to be as objective as possible. For example, a female journalist, commenting on the terrifying number of rapes in the German Federal Republic, noted with some comfort that there were no doubt many more relationships between men and women in which rape was simply unthinkable.

A third factor, once again, is the fear of cultic impurity, fostered by priestly circles especially in the later period. It is not that the female is declared evil or sinful in and of herself, but her otherness, her countervailing power, is seen as an acute danger to the priests' own cultic operation. This attempt at exclusion, sometimes almost hysterical, could easily produce a view of women as "strange" or "evil."

All these factors played a more or less important role in the Judeo-Christian tradition's exclusion of women. From the perspective of the male, who was dominant in religious affairs, women were assigned more to the arena of evil or sin after the institutionalization of monotheism. The story of the fall into sin and its effects (Genesis 3) is a prime example. Zechariah's vision, in which evil incarnates itself as a woman and has to be taken out of the land in a basket sealed with a lead cover (Zech 5:5–11), is along the same line. Partial aspects of this primal male distrust of women show up in the Bible in several places—for example, in the figure of Jezebel (1 Kgs 21:4–7), in Amos's denunciation of the cows of Bashan (Amos 4:1), Isaiah's scolding of the arrogant women of Jerusalem (Isa 3:16–24), or Ezekiel's accusation of the idolatrous prophetesses (Ezek 13:17–23). All this comes together in the many Jewish prejudices against women, which also have their effect in the later writings of the New Testament (1 Tim 2:13–14; 5:11–15). It seems that once female deities and women's religious experience had been set aside, theological reflection about the relationship and the origin of the sexes (generally a male process) could turn against women with fewer inhibitions.

Women became more closely associated with evil, sin, and idols than were men.

As a control, an extensive examination of the religions of other cultures and other times would, of course, be necessary. Without such a comprehensive comparison we cannot answer the question about the degree to which monotheism is responsible for the declining role of women. But for now, a few brief observations must suffice.

In Islam, with its rigorous monotheism, women have, as a rule, fewer public rights than in the Judeo-Christian tradition. Sura 4 of the Qur'an declares: "Men are in charge of women, because Allah hath made the one of them to excel the other" (4:34; trans. M. Pickthall). The exclusion of women from cultic life is also a characteristic of Islam. The woman sometimes has a larger role in Hinduism and Buddhism and enjoys greater respect. But ambivalent male attitudes show up there as well, often leading to contrary appraisals (cf. D. Paul). Brahman superiority is clear in the command: "Even if a husband is void of all virtue, is a slave to desire, and has absolutely no good qualities, a virtuous wife must always honor him as a god" (E. Gerstenberger and W. Schrage, 244, n. 85).

Most African tribal cultures had a patriarchal organization (see H. Loth, who, however, maintains there was a transition from matriarchal to patriarchal rule within the historical period). Similarly, the native cultures of both American continents were for the most part patriarchal (see R. Underhill). For example, in the primarily matrilocal and matrilineal Navajo society, the man has the decisive external role:

> Formally, from the Navaho angle, the "head of the family" is the husband. Whether he is in fact varies with his personality, intelligence, and prestige. Navaho women are often energetic and shrewish. By vigorous use of their tongues they frequently reverse or nullify decisions made by their men. (C. Kluckhohn and D. Leighton, 101)

The role of women is ambivalent here as well, for which the authors just cited have an explanation:

The image of woman, though mostly warm, positive, and full of strength, also has a component of distrust and even of hate which occasionally bursts forth. Is this partly because the mother is the one who at first grants everything but at the age of weaning denies, scolds, and beats away the child who wants the breast? Men are always a little undependable. The father is affectionate to the child, but from the very beginning he comes and goes; the child can never really count on his comfort. Man is fickle—but is never thought to be otherwise. Woman is the one who is either all bad or all good. She gives all or denies all. (Ibid., 199)

South Sea societies were also primarily led by men, though women had and have their own significant religious and social authority, appropriate to their important functions within the family (M. Mead). Finally, despite the common recognition of female deities in Greek and Roman societies and cultures, the depreciation of women existed alongside of and in succession with more liberal tendencies (J. Leipoldt). The shocking disparagement of women by Aristotle and other philosophers proves the thesis that polytheistic worldviews cannot finally protect a culture from the plunge into male monism and discrimination against women.

A preliminary conclusion: The deity has never been, strictly speaking, either male or female. Sexual differentiations within theology are clearly the result of inadequate human imagination. The patriarchal-sexist captivity of the deity arose from a variety of social and historical factors and developments. It was not the result of a unified effort over the millennia of power-hungry males (though this does not excuse us from responsibility for present conditions). Especially in its priestly form, monotheistic faith, which arose in early Judaism, no doubt strengthened already present patriarchal ways of thinking and acting. That is reason enough to reconsider the traditional image of God and to design a theology appropriate for today.

8 | Sexual Roles and the Image of God

We have seen that there is a relation between a culture's social structures and its ideas about God. This correspondence is not, however, so mechanical that a particular social order automatically produces a fixed image of God, or vice versa. Social conditions are too complex to permit such a one-sided perspective— above all, because they are subject to historical change. If we want to inquire about the role of the sexes in today's world and propose an appropriate and legitimate image of God, we will need to consider and compare both the historical development of these issues and the multidimensionality of the present situation.

It is only with the arrival of written records, that is, since the third millennium B.C.E., that we can speak with some certainty about gender-specific tasks and their social assessment. From older archaeological discoveries, grave inscriptions, cave drawings, ruins, and so on we can draw only very cautious conclusions at best. However, with the onset of writing in Mesopotamia and Egypt, the data become more exact. It can be shown that the governing principle in every known culture involved a rough division of labor into inside work for the wife and the female members of the household and outside work for the males (see chapter 6 in this book; also S. de Beauvoir; M. Mead; E. Badinter). This distribution of gender-specific responsibilities grew up over millennia of human history; we must work with it as a given fact. So, our principal questions will be: Is it now necessary, because of the changed social, economic, and political conditions, to give up this ancient division of labor and life? If so, what kind of theology will have to accompany and control these fundamental transformations in society and human personality structures?

Even in Old Testament times the boundaries between male and female areas of activity and responsibility were never completely rigid. Pragmatic give-and-take occurred in both directions. Women were, in fact, sometimes assigned or allowed tasks that ranged far into male territory. To be sure, women are usually described in the Bible by their principle functions (wife or mother) or by their place in the family system (daughter, wife, mother, sister, widow, and so on). Only seldom are they called "mistress" of an estate (1 Kgs 17:17) or "princess" of a region (usually as wife or daughter of the prince: Judg 5:29; 1 Kgs 11:3; Isa 49:23). However, the occupational designations at the royal court depart from the usual practice of limiting women to the care of house and children. According to 1 Sam 8:13 (an appraisal of the monarchy from a later perspective), the court employed women as perfumers, cooks, and bakers. Since even in antiquity men made up the higher ranks of career chefs (cf. Gen 40:1–2) and since, in the later period, purity concerns would definitely have worked against employing women as cooks, this list of occupations suggests some small opening for women during the royal period. Davidic and Solomonic lists of ministers and heroes naturally include no women office holders. Only the queen mother (*gebirah*) exercised a certain traditional and institutional influence at court; the influence of the chief wife of the current king occurred spontaneously, as occasion arose. The "perfumers" mentioned above may, however, have had something to do with ancient religious or magical wisdom. Traces of such knowledge and responsibility are seen at other places in the Old Testament. Joab uses a wise woman from Tekoa to change David's mind (2 Sam 14:2). We have already discussed women soothsayers and prophets. Occasionally, at least, religious and cultic exercises regularly included girls playing tambourines (Ps 68:25 [26]), mourning women (Jer 9:17 [16]), holy women ("temple prostitutes," Hos 4:14), and women temple servants (1 Sam 2:22), not to mention the household religious practices we have assumed for the early period in Israel's history. In sum, the ancient patriarchal order allowed a certain flexibility in the borderline between the sexes. Nevertheless, the course open to either a young man or young woman remained basically determined. Life was shaped by tradition and proceeded along tracks defined by preset switches. Education and socialization prepared children, like their fathers and mothers, for a socially sanctioned order with almost no prospect of change. From their first day of life, they were preprogrammed for certain gender-specific roles (a kind of gender-specific education that, by the way, is still practiced today).

The altered conditions of the industrial age call these traditional roles of the sexes into question. The tragedy of the last two centuries is that the social changes affecting women have been recognized only with great hesitation, and the appropriate social, ecclesiastical, and theological consequences and adjustments have been very slow in coming. To be sure, all this may have less relevance in rural areas; away from the cities the old family structures have tended to maintain themselves—along with their more or less balanced sexual roles. One would also have to consider separately the families of the well-to-do middle class and craftspeople; but the rapidly increasing category of salaried workers, who will soon make up the majority of the industrial urban population, must adapt to completely new ways of life. Women and children, of necessity, are drawn into the processes of production. The separation of living and working space, the impoverishment of large parts of the urban population, and the pulling apart of the family through the different tasks assigned to each of its members characterize a situation that is completely different from that of either present rural culture or any preindustrial society. In industrial society, a woman in the lower social classes no longer has her own household authority. She does not have her own domain—neither in her spatial or physical existence nor in terms of her possessions or her psychic and emotional life. Women are consumed in the family's battle for survival, worn down because they are socially the weakest link in the economically threatened and neglected nuclear family. Here we are speaking primarily of women in the underprivileged majority; and apart from occasional good years and individual successes, the majority of the population in industrial societies remains socially powerless. That is obvious in the extreme in the so-called developing countries that constitute the absolute majority of the world's population. For better or worse, the woman manages her own deprived household, trying to raise the children and doing her best to support her equally oppressed and dependent husband—who, however, can pass his own pressures "down" to his wife. In addition, she tries to increase the family income through her own participation in the process of production, that is, through her own, generally poorly paid, outside job. This system, requiring for women two jobs, one inside the house and one outside, has only rarely brought them more respect; more often it has merely resulted in greater burdens and privations. In sum, the onset of industrialization brought great change to the lives of the majority of the population. The dependence on factory work and machine production robbed the man of the independence he had enjoyed as a farmer and brought the woman into a twofold dependence on her employer and her own husband.

Economic and social transitions of the last two centuries introduced further changes. The entire educational system had to adjust to the demands of a new age. It was no longer sufficient for father and mother to provide their children with the skills the parents had needed in their own predetermined areas of responsibility. Traditional knowledge was no longer enough, no longer able to keep up with the rapid growth of technology. Parental knowledge was already outdated by the time the children were ready to enter the work force. Consequently, a new educational system, administered by the larger society, had to take over the task of preparing the young to assume their roles in industrial production. This was another step toward the incapacitation of the family. Since women were now drawn into the process of production, they, too, increasingly needed a basic education in science and mathematics. Educational programs, earlier sharply separated by gender, became more and more alike. After World War II, Germany adopted a system of basic coeducation for boys and girls— though not without strong debate, especially in ecclesiastical circles. The result of this development is that women, having achieved the same academic and occupational qualifications as men, now demand the same occupational opportunities as well; above all, they see a broad education and the access to occupations with a public or external dimension as indispensable elements of their own personal development. Their demand for economic and occupational equality is fully justified now that the gender-specific division of labor has been set aside. Such demands would have been largely impossible in preindustrial societies, because the material, social, and cultural presuppositions for living autonomously as a woman or man did not exist. Participation in the educational and occupational life of industrial society brings with it quite naturally the demand for participation in shaping, determining, and taking responsibility for the political, economic, and cultural governing bodies and institutions.

Another well-known and hackneyed observation must also be mentioned, one with revolutionary consequences. Until World War I, it was normal for families to have five to ten children. In other words, between ages twenty and forty women experienced an almost unbroken series of pregnancies and deliveries (and a high percentage of women did not live beyond this age). This biological determinism (or must we, in the sense of Gen 3:16, say curse?), which was primarily responsible for keeping women bound to house and hearth, remained in continuous effect into our own century. Only gradually did the means of birth control become more reliable; the desire for smaller families, conducive to the needs of a growing industrial society, become stronger; and social security replaced the care of the aged by "the sons of one's youth" (Ps 127:3–5). In recent decades, women have finally been given the possibility of freedom from successive pregnancies by the discovery of the means to control conception through hormones and other devices. Now, even the deliberate decision never to have children is a real option—an unthinkable idea in the ancient world, because it would have been suicidal.

The revolutionary changes in all aspects of life since the beginning of the industrial age have, of course, brought with them new ways of thinking. Or, one could say with equal validity, the way to the modern world was prepared, set in motion, and made possible by the radically new thinking of the Enlightenment. We do not need to decide this controversy (which came first, the Enlightenment or technical and social changes?) any more than we need to discover whether the roots of autonomous self-consciousness lie in the fifteenth- and sixteenth-century journeys of discovery and colonization, in the biblical demythologizing of the world, or in Greco-Roman rationalism. One thing is certain: the onset of industrialization early in the nineteenth century was marked by a deep break in human life and thought, an upheaval that had immediate effects on women. It seems right to me to see the true beginnings of the women's movement in this historical development, whose effects continue on into our own time. This in no way excludes the fact that discrimination against women already was occasionally recognized as a problem in preindustrial societies, and that emancipation movements sprung up here and there. But it was only the developing industrial society, with its deep structural changes, that prepared the ground for a universal change in consciousness and a broad women's liberation movement.

The "modern" period actually began somewhat earlier as an intellectual development, though one always entangled with societal events, with the awakening of a new self-consciousness. The roots reach far back in human history. It may trace its origins to the developing interest in the individual and to the individual's separation from the collective consciousness of the group that is said to date from the sixth century B.C.E. (see Ezekiel 18), to the credal statements of Paul (see Romans 7–8), to Greek and Roman philosophy, or to the Renaissance. However, the development of a theoretical individualism at the end of the eighteenth century, with its deep effects on concrete social structures, gave a new quality to the desire for self-fulfillment. Philosophical, moral, and religious ideas about the value and basic freedoms of individual human beings, each related directly to God, became politically and socially effective in the declarations of human rights in the United States in 1776 ("All men are created equal, . . . endowed by their Creator with certain unalienable Rights") and in France in 1789. Unfortunately, however, the authors of these declarations, exclusively men of the ruling class, thought of women, slaves, those without property, minors, and dissidents at best only from a patronizing and patriarchal perspective. Nevertheless, the spark of universal human rights had been kindled, applicable to all races, classes, sexes, and ages—a spark that still continues to glow and flicker.

When official documents and speeches continually proclaim universal and individual rights to freedom and human dignity, even the most narrow-minded defender of male domination must finally see that women, too, are human beings who rightfully claim these fundamental rights for themselves. The ideal of personal freedom includes, to no small degree, freedom from gender-determined roles and traditional hierarchies. All people should be able to seek their own self-fulfillment, based on their own gifts and character. Each person should be able to seek her or his own fortune. Determination by others or by outside forces dare no longer obtain. The individual self is a microcosm containing within it all impulses and values. Women's movements want only that women also be allowed to discover their own selves—a goal fully justified by the intellectual environment just described. Self-determination can and dare not apply only to men, exercised at the cost of the "other" sex. Women are independent and responsible subjects, who, like men, must be allowed to take their lives in her own hands. Traditional role stereotypes are no longer normative.

It is obvious how much the economic, social, and psychic realities of the biblical world differ from those of the industrial age. The historical cleft between the two periods simply disallows an unreflective application of biblical and traditional ecclesiastical norms to the contemporary relationship between the sexes and to modern gender roles. The best we can do is compare analogous situations and aspirations, then and now, and, in conversation with the biblical witness, draw appropriate conclusions for the modern era.

Christians cannot act as though the declarations of human rights did not happen. Nor can we repeal the reality of industrialized production and the concomitant striving for individual self-fulfillment. On the other hand, as we have said, the patriarchal missteps of the Judeo-Christian tradition cannot be undone either. What we can do now, though, in responsibility to a liberating God (see chapter 10), is to reconsider theologically the promising and threatening human story, then and now, and put into effect long overdue changes in society and theology toward the end of a common life of human dignity.

Our society dare no longer tolerate standardized behaviors or admission to or prohibition from certain occupations based on gender. The barriers have already been removed in many areas, and women and men often work together without difficulty in the same tasks. Discriminating against women because of their supposed unsuitability for "male occupations" and "male responsibilities" has proven untenable. The only things that remain gender-specific are the biological functions related to conception and birth, and the distribution of voices in the choir. Beyond that, psychology tells us that men and women can freely develop their supposed masculine or feminine "sides," in their relationships with one another and in their common life, to the degree that society permits. But the millennia-old determination of gender roles remains powerful; it is not easily purged from human consciousness.

Two other problems seem to me to be equally important. Both arise from our dialogue with the biblical statements of faith. The first is this: What kind of society can we hope to build, given equal rights for men and women? Do the times require us merely to allow the dominant tendency toward individualized existence to go unchallenged? Should we finally give the reproduction of the race entirely over to laboratory retorts and people-factories, contenting ourselves with short-term human encounters and leaving everything else to autonomous self-fulfillment? Is any kind of common life that goes beyond nonparticipatory coexistence even possible among fully autonomous selves, each dedicated to its own fulfillment? The second question is this: What kind of God would accompany and correct our common life? Strictly speaking, does not every autonomous self demand a unique deity? At the least, must not every identifiable group, stratum, or class have its own divine counterpart?

One thing should be clear: a predetermined role for the sexes in developing their lives—a hierarchical structure—can no longer be tolerated. Overcoming traditional ways of thought and behavior is a requirement of industrialized society; sooner or later this development will, no doubt, have its way. It may even be that it lies in the best interests of industry (and the related centers of power) to isolate and standardize human beings, making them more mobile and more interchangeable (see I. Illich). Already, in many modern production and communication processes, the human is, at best, only a potential disturbance, an unprofitable reality—much too salary-intensive and subject to strikes. Over against such notions stands the deep longing of isolated human beings, each dependent upon the means of production, for meaningful human society (a longing seen in pastoral care and all other forms of human experience). In countless conversations, especially among self-help and experiential groups, the unfulfilled longing for neighborliness, for genuine and lasting relationships, continually reappears. It seems quite impossible to be fully human without these qualities. From the deepest levels of human existence arises an impulse that runs totally contrary to the previously described tendency toward an atomized society. This impulse resonates with the sense of human solidarity and mutual love that we know from the Bible. If this is correct, then the question about the form of a future human common life is justified; then we must go beyond all the various liberation movements and seek the possibility of a new community in a new society. It is insufficient to claim only that once the oppressors are removed from power and the oppressed freed for self-determination, then the wolf will surely graze with the sheep and the child play over the adder's den.

In conversation with the Bible, the question can be posed in this way: Do human solidarity and compassion matter any more, or have they been discredited by the structures of patriarchy and gone the way of the old familial clans? We can, in fact, demonstrate the great distance between the past and the present by examining familial ties. In the biblical period and up to the beginning of the industrial age, the primary concern was for the extended family, despite all patriarchal privilege. Now, we clearly give highest value to the self-fulfillment of the autonomous individual. It would be impossible to turn back this development and, by decree, reconstruct a family structure that would provide us at the same time with full security and absolute freedom. So, now what? What forms will the intimate common life of human beings have to take under the present circumstances? Or can we invent other forms of human community than partnership, family, or living under a common roof?

The outlook for the traditional family structure is not good.

For the most part, it is no longer the nuclear family in which life is celebrated, worked at, or endured. The traditional separation of familial roles provided a way to carry out common tasks. But work, care of the elderly, education, and so on have long since been given over to other social institutions. Many families count themselves lucky if they come together once a day at the breakfast or supper table. For many, even this is impossible. Being together overnight does not compensate for the lack of community and missing the common tasks of the day. Once children reach kindergarten age, it becomes virtually impossible to balance their legitimate personal interests and those of their parents, even with regard to time, place, and transportation; conflicts become inevitable and can scarcely be reconciled. It may be that the best possibilities for mutual accommodation come when young people choose a partner with similar educational and occupational goals, but even then life at work and at home will soon produce a variety of larger or smaller collisions. These arise from the everyday, banal questions about whose career will (for now) take priority, about the distribution of household duties (from cooking and cleaning to shopping and changing diapers), about contacts with friends or groups and leisure-time activities, and from the innumerable trivialities than tend to impinge on the freedom of the other. When the young couple have quite different educational and occupational goals, all kinds of interesting conversational possibilities may open up; but the different interests of each person produce their own dynamics, often resulting in diametrically opposed choices regarding career, where to live, and what to do during free time. Seen in this way, the old distribution of roles according to sex was able to secure and consolidate the earlier family units, whereas the present individualization makes long-lasting partnership virtually impossible. Divorce and separation statistics demonstrate this tendency.

Supporters of the new autonomy of the individual, unless they opt for a strict solipsism, want a democratic structuring of even the smallest human groups. This form of balanced relationship seems, in fact, to offer the only chance for individuals with equal rights to come together as functional social organisms. This solution is impossible without a fundamental willingness to compromise the principle of self-fulfillment with a concern for the other—a necessity for both sexes, not only for women. Biblically speaking, to practice solidarity means to assume responsibility for the group and especially for its weakest members. Biblically speaking, to love the neighbor means, when necessary, to see in the other—especially in the less fortunate—a person of equal or higher value, taking a step back from one's own autonomy. Self-fulfillment becomes secondary to self-limitation and responsibility. This situation is obviously fraught with tension; that tension will continue to characterize the communal forms possible in the future. Experience will soon show to what degree we will, in the future, have to give up on commitments that endure for life (or to what degree we are, thanks to a common change in consciousness, finally freed from them). Experience will also show to what degree same-sex relationships supplant or extend traditional partnerships.

Basic decisions for (or against) new forms of communal life will, of necessity, have their counterpart in our understanding of God. When oppressed minorities break with the traditional Christian image of God they also break with the power elite. Malcolm X used razor-sharp arguments to separate himself from the deity of the "whites" in order to seek the black deity Allah. Radical feminists seek a female basis for existence (see M. Daly) or desire to return to the goddess, apparently because they fear that even appropriate attention to the female elements in the traditional notion of God will only confirm the given male dominance. Such a fear is not without basis. The best integration laws in the United States still have not really opened white society to blacks. But is a break with traditional images of God really a way out for women? It seems to me that the search for the goddess is based in the same old sex-role stereotypes that need to be overcome. The ancient cultures and religions we have tried to understand in this book proceeded from the polarity and complementarity of the sexes both in heaven and on earth. Along with preexilic Israel, they saw this complementarity as balanced, mutually related, and holistic—precisely not as dualistic and antagonistic, denigrating one side or the other. The dualistic and mutually exclusive perspective arose only from a superior, priestly, "men's club" mentality, which in the course of Christian history celebrated many an unfortunate triumph. This dualistic view blocked the way to mutuality by despising the other; it tried to deal with its own self-alienation through alienation of others, thinking love can be engendered through hatred of the other. Should this view now be encouraged by denying the "male" god and worshiping the goddess instead? Is it so impossible for women to find some kind of community with the ruling male elite in their entrenched roles that they need the autonomous goddess for support? Must a "dead" male theology first be replaced by a "life-giving" goddess before a new, harmonious community of the sexes will once again be possible? Do the gradual changes in the direction of equal rights for women and the disintegration of the male stereotypes for God count for nothing?

As briefly stated earlier, the most liberating possibility, as I see it, is to hold fast to the monotheism of old. At least in theory, belief in one God includes the greatest possible openness to the justified claims of equality of all people. Those who project into the heavens the inequality they themselves seek to overcome always create new barriers. A plurality of deities contradicts the principle of equality because it gives new theological life to the differences that must be overcome. Fundamentally, however, the prevailing image of God is largely determined by the reality of experience, not by logic or theory. A society open to both sexes will also have a deity (or several gods and goddesses?) that is (are) equally accessible to all. Such a deity will correspond to the mysterious longing for solidarity and compassion known to all humans, and, contrary to the spirit of the times, remind those addicted to autonomy of their common humanity.

9 | *Women and the Church*

Male and female feminist theologians correctly point out the close relationship between the status of women in the church and the nature of the God the church proclaims. The relation between the image of women and the image of God is, of course, complex; it is mutually affected from both sides rather than solely determined by only one image or the other. But the fundamental rule is frighteningly true: the more the community of faith is ruled exclusively by men, the more quickly male interests and prejudices are reflected in the church's theology and the more easily the alien notions of God thus produced affect the structure of the religious community; these then serve to legitimize male domination and the disenfranchisement and exclusion of women from religious responsibility. In the name of a sole, jealous, male God, it is possible for unequally privileged males to devalue women with impunity. It is a sign of an unpardonable lack of discernment on the part of the church leadership that even into our own century theologians of the stature of Karl Barth can hold rigidly to the subordination of women as an unchangeable order of creation and redemption.

Some will challenge the preceding premise, arguing perhaps that men have too high a regard for women's compassion and solicitude to exclude them from the church. They may point to the Catholic cult of Mary as proof. But that argument underestimates the egoism and willfulness of a group of people anxiously holding on to positions of privilege. An increasingly multicultural modern society, with its loss of the sense of security provided by belonging to the intimate group, strengthens the tendency toward isolation and self-assertion. Feminist theologians correctly point out that the idealization of female solicitude and devotion, even in the form of Mary as "queen of heaven," serves to keep women in a subordinate position (see R. Ruether, 171ff.).

It has been sufficiently documented that women have been and remain more or less excluded from active and responsible partici- pation in the cultic and public religious life of Christianity, Juda- ism, and Islam. On the basis of ancient social patterns, women have been and continue to be relegated to the hands-on internal work of ecclesiastical and diaconal service. There they have al- ways been welcome. But women have found great difficulty in gaining access to the tasks of congregational and churchwide leadership and to their share of responsibility in theological edu- cation and church governance. Women make up the core of the congregation at Sunday worship; they provide the personnel for the women's societies and constitute the majority of the commit- tees and interest groups. But for the most part they remain under- represented in leadership bodies, to say nothing of the theological schools and disciplines. It was, for example, very difficult in the 1960s to find women candidates for the office of elder in German congregations. Even women who were very active in the congre- gation and interested in the task faced inner inhibitions stemming from the old gender-role stereotypes—or were strongly advised against or even prohibited from such activity by their husbands, "for the sake of the family." In 1988, it was still deemed worthy of special mention in Germany that, after intensive consciousness- raising among the laity, women won 40 to 50 percent of the seats in local Catholic church councils. Nevertheless, comparing these events does show a positive development over the last decades. But there still remain many "pure" male theological institutions that have only begun thinking about these matters. On the one hand, there are not yet enough qualified women to apply for the job openings; on the other hand, in many places the same old male self-righteousness and presumption of male technical com- petence still reign.

Fundamentally, one can say that the imbalance between the sexes had come already with the establishment of monotheism. Women were robbed of their own areas of religious responsibility. In the male communities of faith, women were given at best a seat off to the side or in the balcony. This religious disenfranchisement of women should never have happened. It becomes particularly obvious and intolerable today with the struggles for equal rights in the larger society, while archaic structures and patterns of thought continue in church and theology. We must confront the long overdue question: How can men and women reform ecclesiastical structures so women are able to exercise their proper voice and responsibility? Or must we ask, more radically, How can the church become what it has essentially been already for a long time—a women's church? All the democratic rules by which our society supposedly functions lead to one conclusion: the church belongs to women, because it consists primarily of women!

However, since Christian women have primarily waged their struggles individually, without a common organization that might have given notice to churches, church councils, synodical offices, and theological societies, they have had to take the long route, entering the institutions from the bottom.

In this connection, we raise here only a few significant preliminary questions. The central problem among the Catholic, Orthodox, and in some places the Anglican churches is the admission of women to the priestly office. Arguments against the equal treatment of the sexes are finally based in the old role stereotypes: women have their own social and religious vocation, which, however, is different from that of men. Women's vocation does not include dealing with the sacrament of the altar. Jesus and his disciples only admitted males to the administration of this sacrament. The decisive factor lying behind such argumentation, whose imprudent assertions obviously offend against the modern democratic consciousness, is the millennia-old male tradition of hunting and sacrifice and its taboo against female contact with the sacrificial blood. W. Burkert has tried to explain the origins of this male sacrificial privilege on the basis of stone-age hunting practices. Christians have to understand that even ecclesiastical customs and ordinances, including the Eucharist, were shaped by the forms of an earlier time and are, therefore, subject to change. It is not at all clear that the administration of this sacrament was limited to men in the earliest Christian communities. At any rate,

the circle of people around Jesus and the early church, in expectation of the coming kingdom of God, demonstrated such lack of
concern for old rules and constraints that this period of church
history still retains a provocative and liberating influence (see E.
Moltmann-Wendel, *Land;* L. Schottroff). Why can't Christians
bring this same liberating influence to bear on the final years of
the twentieth century? Why don't they emerge from the shadows
of obsolete traditions and unreflected millennia-old blood taboos
and say courageously that women have the same rights as men,
even with regard to the sacrament of the altar? If the contemporary need for women priests seems unconvincing and the reference to parallels in religious history are disallowed, they could
always point to the biblical example of Zipporah (Exod 4:26).

In biblical and other religious traditions, the taboo connected
with the word has never been as strong as that associated with the
sacrificial blood. To be sure, there have been attempts to make
the holy word the secret possession of a particular caste. But since
both sexes are equally capable of speech and both make use of
language in their respective areas of work, the church never had
such an irrational prohibition regarding the ministry of proclamation as the one regarding sacrifice. Since the end of World War
II, women in many Protestant churches have succeeded in entering the pastoral office, where they have demonstrated to astonished congregations and elite groups of males that women oversee
the pastoral office not worse than men, but better. The old male
attitudes of mistrust and hostility (to which there are also corresponding and opposite female attitudes), which asserted that a
particular profession is not for women, that "they" could never
manage it, could be overcome only by experiential data. Only statistics are able to show the skeptics (those willing to think about
it) that women drivers, physicians, and politicians are not less valuable than men in comparable positions merely because of their
sex. Male prejudice, fed by ancient stereotypes, gives way only to
demonstrable reality. That is true in the church as well. In many
places, women pastors have now gained the respect of the majority of people. There is once again good reason to point to the
female prophets in the Old Testament and to the blossoming liberation of women in the time of Jesus and the early church. In

other places the Old Testament speaks of the equality of the sexes in its visions of the future: "Then afterward I will pour out my spirit on all flesh; your sons and your daughters shall prophesy" (Joel 2:28 [3:1]). "For the LORD has created a new thing on the earth: a woman encompasses a man" (Jer 31:22). Thus, there is a sense in the biblical tradition that the preeminence of men over women in synagogue and church runs seriously afoul of the dignity of both sexes. It is time to correct this mistake, whether or not the end time has arrived. Contemporary social conditions and the ancient Israelite-Judeo-Christian proclamation of a liberating God require equal status for women. As the word is proclaimed in congregations in which women pastors exercise their office without challenge, this goal is already within reach.

But the situation is different in congregational and synodical leadership and in the world of theology. At the highest levels of congregational and denominational administration, men still set the tone, often without the refinement of even a single token woman. It is strange, actually, that men are comfortable in this "chemically pure" male atmosphere. The widespread debate about the status of women must make clear to them that women everywhere, as an underrepresented group, are demanding full participation in life and thought, in making judgments and decisions. Biblically and in Christian teaching, women have a right to nothing less. Why would a church whose foundation is built on women want to do without women in its decision-making and governing bodies? Why doesn't the ruling male elite in theological education make energetic attempts to grant equal voice and responsibility to women? Why aren't laws, institutions, and customs that hinder women's full participation in the life of the church changed more quickly and more decisively? Why do we still so often hear threadbare arguments asserting the lack of suitability of women for theology and church leadership? It is very simple for us to recognize and denounce the insensitivity of the white South African elite or the Latin American landowners over against people who are landless and deprived of rights. But these injustices occur in faraway lands. The log in one's own eye is often harder to recognize than the speck in the eye of the other.

Despite all the difficulties on the way to equal rights, the old

distribution of roles according to gender will finally prove outdated even in the church, and women will assume their rightful
places. What will this mean for our understanding of God? Will
our all-too-human constructions for speaking about God—the
male attributes and characteristics that appear in our prayers, lit-
urgies, and theological descriptions—lose their male character?
In the future, will God be portrayed as less majestic, jealous,
vengeful, punitive, judging, and killing, and instead more loving,
understanding, forgiving, suffering, and open? Such an adjust-
ment of gender-dependent qualities in the image of God is conceivable. But to the degree that role stereotypes disappear in the
larger society, old human projections on the divine image will also
lose their power. Then one might expect theological statements
that encompass both male and female realities (that are, in other
words, human) about God's power and authority, tolerance and
solicitude. Must they, though, be fundamentally different from
today's theological statements? (We have always had the witness
to God's compassion in, say, Hos 11:1–9 and Jer 31:20.)

All of this raises the question of the particular contributions of
women and men in today's church and in the construction of our
image of God. An answer requires a somewhat fuller clarification
of the bases from which such questions can be asked and an-
swered. Feminist theology often speaks emphatically of a female
spirituality, which, having been suppressed for centuries, must
now be brought to light and given its own validity. What is a specifically "female spirituality"? We need to make a fundamental
decision here. Are we going to assume there are irreconcilable
natural characteristics peculiar to each gender, or merely that
there are functional and cultural differences in sexual roles given
by gender-specific socialization? Are human beings, from the moment the embryo becomes sexually differentiated, forced into determined gender-specific behaviors, or are human role patterns
acquired in the first years of life, that is, externally imprinted? In
the first case, we would affirm a predetermined dualism that goes
far beyond the polarity of the sexes operative in the biblical period. In the second case, we would have to do with biological differentiation that occurs within the framework of a common human heritage, leaving open considerable room for adjustments

and changes in male and female behavior. The starting point will manifestly influence the results of our discussion. It seems to me that the ancient cultures proceeded for the most part from a polarity of the sexes that was in no way essentially dualistic. The role crossovers of Deborah, Jael, and others in the Old Testament argue for a pragmatic interpretation of gender polarity. To be sure, later developments, especially in postexilic priestly thought, did require an ontological and dualistic opposition of male and female. This contrast was cemented ever more securely in the patriarchal reflections of the Greek and Judeo-Christian tradition. The man was the true human; the woman his opposite, or a complementary or even deficient being. By nature, she was unable to achieve the degree of perfection of the image of God found in the male; thus, she was sometimes seen as nothing less than a negative counterpart of the male. Even the priestly theologian in Gen 1:27 does not imply the equality of the sexes; at least in cultic perspective, he maintains the qualitative difference between them that he presents throughout the priestly document (Gen 5:1–2; 6:19–20; 7:2–8; Lev 16:3–10). All conscious forms of patriarchal superiority live from the strict differentiation of the sexes and the supposed biological inferiority of the woman. Those who, on the contrary, now want to emphasize the naturally given qualities of the female, which remain psychically and physically unachievable by men, move in the same ontological categories as the clearly defined patriarchy. "Female spirituality" sometimes seems to take on the characteristics of such an ontological category in feminist literature—except, of course, that now it is positively valued and its male counterpart negatively valued. The consequence to be drawn seems to be that church and world can be healed only by the female nature. Such a reversal of the traditional male worldview is in no way surprising. Perhaps it takes this kind of radical antithesis to shake male self-consciousness. But the thesis of a qualitative superiority of one gender cannot be removed or contradicted by the antithesis of an essential higher valuation of the other—one claim merely replaces the other. Both assertions or worldviews are plainly false. They absolutize partial aspects of a complementary reality.

The women's movements of the nineteenth and twentieth centuries have not been based in an ontological dualism of the sexes but rather in the presupposition that women are people of equal value, and as such claim equal dignity and equal rights in society. From the biblical perspective we can add that women, like the oppressed peoples of the "third" and "fourth" world, can offer a depth of human wisdom deriving from their millennia-long experience of suffering and a socialization grounded in enforced subordination. Female spirituality, like the spirituality of the base communities of Latin America, is a ferment renewing church and society. It lives from the desire for and the experience of loving human relationships free of violence. In this way, women, as the oppressed and suffering majority of the population, have the opportunity to contribute to healing the world from war and oppression. Only those who have themselves experienced mistreatment know how inhumane the domination of some people by others really is; they alone may perhaps be able to correct the mistakes of a history that, up to now, has been guided by men.

In my opinion, the dualistic division of the world into good and evil ways of being, good and evil groupings of people or genders, social classes, peoples, or social systems is always a dangerous mistake. Biological, anthropological, and social-scientific observations argue instead for the assumption that we become women and men only in the course of our childhood development, begun with the relatively slow differentiation of the embryos and moving to a gender-specific and culturally different socialization as male and female members of society. In today's world, actual biological differences play only a minimal role in predetermining employment possibilities for women and men. We have already seen that up until the beginning of the modern era biological factors were much more strongly responsible for the distribution of roles between the sexes.

"Femininity" is largely the result of role stereotypes shaped and determined by patriarchy. There was a reason for German psychologist Margarete Mitscherlich to urge women no longer to turn their aggressions inward against themselves, as demanded by patriarchal rules, but instead to turn them outward, like men. Accordingly, "female spirituality" is that experience of God and human beings won by women throughout Christian history through their pain, privation, and manifold suffering. Theologically, women's spirituality, like that of the poor, is the church's most valuable treasure, since, in biblical perspective, a true relationship with God and true Christian formation are found, paradoxically, in distress and alienation rather than in positions of power (see Matt 5:3–12; 1 Peter 4). The history of the church—indeed, the history of piety in all religions—offers countless examples of this. We need only remind ourselves of black spirituality in the United States and South Africa. The modesty, openness, and human solidarity—in other words, the love—so bitterly lacking today in the churches of the industrialized world can only be learned from the bottom up or in movement toward the bottom. Ecclesiastical and social attempts to achieve security though domination and affluence are, on the contrary, guaranteed to prevent the spiritual renewal offered in the biblical message (see A. Tevoedjre; J. Hinkelammert).

If women are willing to remain at all in a male church, to hold any hope for it rather than to turn away in disappointment and found their own religious sisterhoods (a very regrettable but very real possibility), they will have to propose their spiritual perceptions to the church more strongly than Hildegard von Bingen or Theresa von Avila were able to do in their own time. On the other hand, the ruling male elite will have to give free rein to female spirituality at the expense of their own lust for domination. They will have to learn from it as from a Christian demeanor refined by affliction. Jesus, the Christ, finally modeled a life of humility, always pointing to the weak and helpless as examples of the kingdom of God. He looked toward those at the bottom and urged his followers to learn from those below, from the small and the helpless. He even called upon people to associate with these weak and lowly ones. Women come from those at the bottom, more so in the church than in many secular areas. The evangelical task of the church, therefore, is to join in solidarity with women, just as with all others who are among the lowly.

What can the church learn today? What must it learn? It lives always under the temptation to lift itself triumphantly above other people, other religious and social groups. It is always drawn into the universal striving for profit and success, the need for recognition, and the false trust that everything can be manipulated. Women, so long oppressed, know that force, power, and the desire for prestige corrupt both humanity and the message of Jesus Christ; in fact, that these drives, in their contemporary excess, lead to the abyss. Oppressed people recognize this more clearly than rulers and profit-makers. Throughout Christian history, women have, of necessity and of their own will, been closely associated with the diaconate. Once the rule of men in the diaconal office (see Acts 6:1–6) was overcome, countless numbers of women have been employed in the diaconal service of Christian congregations and church bodies. As ordered sisters and deaconesses, as pastor's wives, administrative employees, catechists, workers in social ministries, and honorary office-holders, they have embodied the church's serving function. They have borne the full brunt of the practical work in congregations, always having to bow to the rules of the "superior" male theologians and ecclesiastical hierarchy. They have had to work under the direction of a "Herr Pastor," often acting against their own better judgment won in the trenches. I remember well the four deaconesses in our congregation. Often they had the better and deeper practical and theological insights. But we pastors set the guidelines for the work of the parish. Finally, of course, as paradoxical as it sounds, we must be thankful for the history of diaconal work in the Christian church despite its unpardonable discrimination against women. But this thankfulness dare not be misused. It would be wrong to confine women, with their willingness to help, to tasks of service. On the contrary, the church, up to the highest levels, must be renewed on the basis of women's diaconal experience, that is, renewed from below. Service, not power, is the leading motif for Christian men and women (see Matt 20:25–28; John 13:14–15). The history of service to the neighbor and others, with women taking the major role, has done much more to preserve the evangelical commission to proclaim salvation and peace and to practice love and solidarity than all theological utterances and controlling ambitions of the men of the church. The service of women to the neighbor, both near and far, matches the biblical commission given to the entire congregation. The spirituality deriving from the service to the neighbor is more important today than ever for the church and, beyond the church, for the industrial society that has given itself shamelessly to an ideology of affluence and power. The public face of the church has, to a large degree, followed the operative principles of society. Its primary concern has been its diminishing numbers and decreased income. Female spirituality, in contrast, stands in direct continuity with the biblical ethos of love of neighbor. The piety of the poor in the Psalter (see Psalm 37), the veneration of the servant of God in Second Isaiah (Isa 52:13—53:12), the modesty taught by the wisdom literature (see Prov 30:7–9), even the ancient family ethos itself (see Lev 19:9–18)—not to mention the beatitudes in the Sermon on the Mount (Matt 5:3–10), the example of Jesus (see Matt 20:25–28; John 12:1–17), and the teaching of the early church (see Gal 6:1–3; 1 Cor 10:23–24)—all point in the same direction. To a surprising degree, all the Bible's communal ethical reflections are other-directed. This ethical alignment derives, of course, from sensitive men, just like most of the biblical writings. The biblical ethos, in all its historical and social forms, is a community-producing ethos. It derives from the small family group, from centuries of oppression, and from suffering that spans the generations. That is why it turns away from power, force, and caprice, seeking instead love, peace, and understanding with the neighbor. The experiences of women, suffered during millennia of second-class citizenship, fit seamlessly with this biblical ethos, as long as they keep the other person in view and keep love of neighbor as their foundation and goal. When, in the heat and bitterness of the struggle for emancipation, the discovery of the self becomes the most urgent goal, conflicts with the Christian tradition will arise. But are the search for self-identity and the love of neighbor mutually exclusive aspirations? As we have seen, in biblical perspective, one depends on the other.

The virtues claimed exclusively for women in many feminist writings, namely, integrated existence, peacemaking, human solidarity, warmth, and openness, are in large measure enjoined in the Bible for all, binding on the entire community. Those characteristics unmasked today as male—the desire for power and success, aggressiveness in church and society—are seen in large measure in the Bible as human misbehavior, destructive of com munity. The church's diaconal service has, to be sure, been the primary domain of women, but never their sole possession. Men, too, have always been involved in the work of service as an expression of the gospel. In Christian congregations, the distinction between internal and external tasks has never been determined absolutely by the differentiation of the sexes. Thus, comparing women's internal service to men's traditional external leadership is one-sided. It must be expanded by the parallel presentation of men and women in the church who have exercised the same functions of service and administration. The error of attempting to divide cleanly between good and bad behavior, ascribing the one to women and the other to men, actually derives from a dualistic worldview that is fundamentally patriarchal in origin; it partakes of an absolutized division of labor, with women called to the lower tasks of service and men to higher ecclesiastical responsibilities. Fortunately, this principle has never been practiced in the church's history or consequently proposed in theory. It is no more correct if turned around: the woman is good and superior, the man bad and inferior. The feminist rebellion is understandable: the ruling elite in the church, as in economics and politics, has for millennia consisted of men, who have increasingly pursued aggressive science, technology, and the structures of economics, society, and the bureaucratic church (see D. Sölle). Nevertheless, a dualistic contrast between a female spirituality and a self-destructive male hunger for power is false. The undesirable tendencies in modern church and society have not developed from male genes, but from society's distribution of functions. Women have sporadically participated in aggressive and imperialistic affairs. Women have never been kept totally separate, and have now and then also promoted such negative tendencies, either quietly or actively. That is less clear in the public work of the church than in the economic and political institutions of society, though in general we can say that wherever women have shared responsibility they have conducted themselves like human beings, that is, sometimes with solidarity and love, and sometimes seeking domination, power, and success. There are striking examples in which women leaders have promoted peace, but men, too, have sometimes functioned as genuinely peaceful rulers. History has also known female bloodthirsty tyrants. Even one such example would call into question the assertion of a female goodness given by nature itself. But there are many examples, and the daily experiences of life demonstrate clearly that women are "by nature" capable of evil. Similar internal or external communal responsibilities produce in both men and women very similar human behavior, both good and ill (compare, for example, the existence of both male and female nurses and teachers).

Moreover, in the life of the church—apart from and sometimes in contradiction to church doctrine—we have seen communities under traditional male leadership that have nevertheless been open and nonaggressive places of peace and good will. Now it may be that one needs a magnifying glass to find these in European and American industrial societies; as a result, they have escaped notice in the northern hemisphere by feminist theologians. However, in the southern hemisphere (under oppression by the North), such ecclesiastical communities are more clearly observable; and even if they do not fully meet all idealistic expectations, their very existence contradicts the bald assertion that churches and congregations run by men can act only self-destructively, egocentrically, and chauvinistically—or that, where they exhibit a more human face, it has been stolen from women. I think of churches and dioceses that stand in solidarity with the poor from the top down, that have given up power and possessions or placed them completely in the service of the poor. Helder Camara, Everisto Arns, Pedro Casaldaliga, Adriano Hipolito, Jose Maria Pires, Oscar Romero, Eduardo Pironio, and Leonidas Proana are bishops and archbishops of the holy Roman Catholic Church who have relinquished only the smallest part of their traditional male orientation; yet these men stand for the best biblical and evangelical tradition of solidarity with the poor—giving the self in the service of the other and renouncing power and possessions. There is no way to explain their actions by sociology or psychology. According to common expectations and functional theories of the use of power, they should act in precisely contrary ways, demonstrating the authority and presumption of their high office. But they do the opposite. These bishops, men who are sensitive to the humanity of "the least brother and sister," exhibit an uncommon

personal charisma that is often paired with poetic vitality and con-
tagious humor. This is nothing short of miraculous, since such
men offend not only against tradition but against all the rules of
social science. True, they have not broken down all the barriers
of "machismo." There are, for example, no women priests in offices equal to theirs. But, though bound by tradition, they live
out and demonstrate a fundamental liberated openness in their
theological thought and churchly practice that makes one forget
their human frailties. Their ecclesiastical leadership style employs
both militant and compassionate energy for the liberation of the
oppressed. And if, in their battle for the liberation of those who
are economically and politically disenfranchised, they have not
yet fully appreciated that in the midst of the class struggle there
is also the particular oppression of women, then, viewed from a
distance, we might call that another human frailty. The women's
issue carries less weight in their world because the economic and
political oppression is so overwhelming. Scarcely anyone in Latin
America, male or female, would support the claim of many feminists that sexist oppression is the root of all evil. That dubious
honor seems to belong to a form of economic exploitation inherent in industrial societies and interwoven in all levels of society.
The human capacity for oppression most likely arose first not in
the family but at secondary levels of social organization.

Some Latin American dioceses and many base communities
exhibit, therefore, a potential for liberation within the church that
might also remove the oppression of women, and in some places
already has. Does not a church with this orientation approach the
ideal described, for example, by Mary Daly (among others) as the
"cosmic sisterhood"? Integration of the unfolding person, without the negation of contradictions; genuine human relationships;
a truly equal community of all people; a healing prophetic function exercised by the church; active nonviolent struggle for the
oppressed; joy in one another and in common meditation and
work; community-building worship; unhindered participation in
and assistance with the sacrament; a fundamental place in the
community for creativity, imagination, and humor; freedom from
anxiety; mutual trust and love—these are characteristics of the
community enjoined from the beginning in the biblical witness.

They can actually be found among the base communities of Latin America, just as they were among the disciples of Jesus and in the early Christian church. Dualistic slogans ("Female spirituality is life-affirming; male engagement produces only death") simply ignore this reality.

The image of God in feminist theology is based heavily on the biblical foundation of the mercy and faithfulness of Yahweh. However, God's power and aggressiveness, God's punishment, judgment, and rule, are rightly reconsidered and relativized. The same is true in the liberation theologies of Latin America and Africa. Feminist theologians also rightly push for a rediscovery of the "female" dimensions of the notion of God. They point, for example, to the third article of the Christian faith, with its traditions of the spirit of God, the church, and the people of God, all of which were portrayed as feminine in the ancient world (E. Moltmann-Wendel, *Land*, 98–99; E. Sorge). The personhood of God has also come under discussion. It is not only in Buddhist tradition that the antagonistic contradictions arising from the world's division into autonomous individual egos must be overcome to achieve full perfection. With the loss of the personhood of God, any temptation to envision God as a sexually determined being would automatically disappear. Judeo-Christian theology actually has no absolute and unchangeable, predetermined, and fixed predication of God. Consequently, all ideas of God, including those that come from the experience of oppressed peoples and oppressed women, are open to discussion in the church. On the other hand, definitions of God cannot be the "work" of just one man or one woman. They are subject to the mutual criticism of others who seek and respond to God, and they must confront the historical credal affirmations of our forefathers and foremothers in the faith (cf. Hebrews 11—even this patriarchal list of faithful witnesses contains two women). It is extraordinarily important, indeed, of greatest urgency, that all theological statements of the church now be formulated only with the equal participation of knowledgeable and committed women. This is often already possible in church conventions, governing bodies, councils, and presbyteries. But more than 90 percent of the chairs of theology in German seminaries and universities are still occupied by men. Up to now, women theologians have had only minimal chances, and perhaps no great motivation, to penetrate this theological hierarchy. Yet their participation in this area, too, is essential. Intensive promotion of graduate study for women and, if necessary, the use of quotas are needed to reach this goal.

In addition to the experience of oppression they share with many underprivileged men, women bring to church and theology also their unique biological existence. This has always been just as strange to men as the sexual dimension of men remains to women. As a rule, each sex can only speak of the other on the basis of observation and association, not from its own experience. Judgments about the other sex, therefore, can be made only cautiously. One thing is clear: if the church is to exercise true equality of the sexes in theory and practice, the biological realities of both women and men must be given equal weight. Despite the widespread functional equality of the sexes in social and cultural contexts, the menstrual cycle, conception, pregnancy, birth, and nursing of infants remain specifically female realities, just as male hormonal makeup and basic male sexual behavior represent specifically masculine modes of existence. And just as male sexuality has always been significant for theology and church, now—as part of a genuine rehabilitation of women in the church—female sexuality must also inform the image of God. Men's lamenting that such thinking opens the floodgates to "other gods," contravening the first commandment, or that it dishonors the one God, offers no help at all. Their complaint merely butts up against the convincing feminist argument that the Bible's prohibition of foreign gods and graven images has forever been de facto transgressed by men in a sexist manner. So what remains is either a justified female transgression of the commandment to match that of men or a fundamental reworking or even totally new formulation of the doctrine of God. The latter possibility will be considered in chapter 10. For now, I want to use one more example to demonstrate the problem of female attributes of the deity.

The beginning of the Bible contains two creation stories (Genesis 1–2). Both are formulated from a male point of view. In the older narrative, God is a handworker who forms the male human being out of the earth, breathes life into him, and then makes a "helper" corresponding to him out of his own body (Gen 2:4b–25). God is *homo faber*, a creator who, like a man, works with his hands—the only material and creative way men know how to work. In accord with male patriarchal understanding, the male is the first human creature; the woman, who is subordinate to him, comes only later. This view reflected the contemporary social structure and mentality. The younger narrative (Gen 1:1—2:4a) speaks of creation through the word (see Ps 33:6–9). Academically educated men, used to giving commands (in this case, priests), are capable of such a notion. Both creation stories are an insult to today's self-conscious woman, perhaps also to many women of the preindustrial period who were thinking beyond their own culture. Why is the most elemental, life-giving event—emergence from the egg, from the body of the mother, giving birth—not included in the primeval event? Can't it serve as an analogy for divine creation? Why, according to the Bible, is the world created twice, but both times through male generation, never born from the female womb? There are indications, though minimal ones, that the birth of the world and humanity from a primal uterus was an idea known also in Israel. Ps 90:2 states, "Before the hills were yet born and earth and the dry land were lying in pains of birth" (trans. H.-J. Kraus, 212). Ps 139:15 also presupposes the birth of the (first?) human being in the primeval mother earth: "when I was being made in secret, intricately woven in the depths of the earth." (See also the notion of a primal womb in Job 38:8, 29.) Stories of the primeval mother were, therefore, present in Israel in one mythological form or another, but they were overlaid and repressed by purely male experiences of forming, making, and commanding. In the Old Testament period, when the traditions of faith were living and developing, this male form of the creation narrative would not have been so serious. Faith and cultic life were determined by life as it was experienced, by countless oral traditions (now lost), and perhaps even by particular female cultic legends defining areas of women's religious responsibility. But once written down and canonized, the biblical texts took on normative authority. Life became limited by the guidelines established in Scripture. Prior to the written Bible, female oral traditions and an independent female cultic practice were still thinkable. But in fixing a written Scripture, male texts became dominant, because only men were involved in the process of producing the biblical literature.

It is impossible to compensate for this decisive defect in the written theological bequest left to us by the people of Israel and the early Christian church by the occasional use of female divine attributes, such as "mercy" (derived from word for "womb"; see Jer 31:20), "spirit" (Gen 1:2), or "mother" (Isa 66:13; on this question, see P. Trible, *Rhetoric*). The sexual metaphors of the Old Testament are already so generalized or so absorbed into patriarchal thought that they cannot be regarded as representative of female theology. To some degree, they show only that in the patriarchal society of that day, female religion could easily be integrated into masculine cultic language. Female religiosity was not suppressed, nor was it excluded as dangerous or polluting; it was taken up into male notions of faith. However one imagines it (see chapter 5), male and female forms of religion existed side by side in the early period of Israel's history. The profane Song of Songs can serve as witness to this one-time balance of the sexes within the patriarchal structures.

After the elimination of the female cult and after the social upheaval of modern times, it is necessary to compensate for the lack of female theological substance. It is untenable that ideas of God based only on male concepts continue to govern our theology. Biblical faith is chiefly the faith of the powerless and the oppressed. Their experiences of God—not those of the powerful elite—have been preeminent in shaping the portrayal of God. That is true from Moses and the Hebrew slaves to the prophets, who sympathized with the marginal groups, to Jesus, who himself came from the lowest class. Out of their own hopes, the weak and the poor created the picture of a just, powerful, retributive, and, above all, loving God. They, along with their laments and their confessions of trust, have been lifted up in biblical theology. Now that we are aware of the situation of women, they too—as a specific majority among those who cry "out of the depths"—must find their rightful place in theology.

10 | *The Liberating God*

Theological pronouncements have never been simple. They seek to clarify the ground and goal of existence, to explain origins and meaning and death and life. Such statements raise truth-questions more intensely than other forms of human speech. They seek to orient, enable, and safeguard faith, the basic human trust. Therefore, the truth or falsehood of our theology has much to do with whether we succeed in life or fail. Theology, along with its secular counterparts—worldview, ideology, superstition, esotericism—is necessary to the survival of individuals and society. A false theology produces death; a correct theology supports life.

The proper knowledge of God is a central problem in the biblical writings of every period. Who is God, and what does God require of human beings? Within the web of the prevailing social and political order, the Bible discusses the possibility of missing or disdaining the true intentions and dimensions of God with surprising fullness and clarity. The biblical testimonies are concerned with recognizing the true God and unmasking the false gods, that is, gods that are incompetent and ineffective and that do not enhance life. The common denominator of all criticism of false gods, domestic and foreign, is the recognition that human beings, overestimating their own abilities, invent a deity, desiring to hitch it to the wagon of their own egoistic or group interests. The biblical witnesses see the relation of humans to the deity primarily under the rubric of power. That which lies behind what Horst Eberhard Richter has described as the modern mania for self-assertion and autonomy, or behind what we know in the contemporary discussion about human survival as the problem of controlling atomic energy, space travel, and gene technology, was already known in the Old Testament: human beings, because they are human, grab for the highest power. They want to be like God (Gen 3:5; 11:6). On the basis of present knowledge, can we say that men alone fall victim to this lust for power? The biblical witness indicts people of both sexes. As long as men were primarily entrusted with the external public representation of the group, the maintenance and extension of power naturally fell mainly in their area of responsibility. In the view of the biblical authors, however, when sexual roles were reversed, women were immediately subject to the same temptation. The examples of Queen Jezebel (1 Kings 21) and Athaliah (2 Kings 11) demonstrate that quite well. In my opinion, historical experience and modern empirical research confirm the fact that aggression and hunger for power among men and women are not of a different kind, but are distinguishable from one another only in their nuances and direction (cf. M. Mitscherlich; cf. chapter 8). However, the fact that men, as those primarily responsible for "wanting to be like God," try to shift the responsibility to women is, to be blunt, a sign of cowardice and meanness (see the Grimm brothers' fairy tale "The Fisherman and His Wife"). It is only Genesis 3 that introduces the role play of the sexes as a way to explain the presence of evil in the world. From there, the women's alleged manipulation has had a one-sided and unwarranted effect in the history of theology. But the other "fall" stories in Genesis 1–11 or Ezek 28:11–19 speak entirely differently about the coming of evil. In Genesis 4, it is the quarrel between the first two brothers that suggests the dangerous possibilities lurking in human nature and that sets in motion the fateful murder of the brother. Or, again, it is the heavenly beings who are responsible for the titanic forces of history by engaging in intercourse with human women (Gen 6:1–4). Or, urban life seduces human beings into overstepping their already significant power by seizing heaven (Gen 11:1–9). The story of Adam and Eve should never have been interpreted in isolation. At the very least, the various accents of the other "fall" stories that follow the Eden narrative in the Mosaic primeval history should have been given equal status as sources for a theology of sin and evil. Perhaps a sense of balance requires us today to include the modern myth of the patriarchal conspiracy against women's religious experience in this series of primal narratives about the origin of evil.

According to the biblical witness, the impulse toward absolute autonomy is a chief reason for missing the true God and distorting the divine image. In its long history, Israel experienced several crucial moments of false worship. For example, the worship of the powers or gods of nature brings with it the danger of forgetting the God of historical deliverance and social justice (see Hosea 2; Jeremiah 2). Or, again, economic power befuddles people into behaving like unassailable autocrats (see Ezekiel 27–28). As a result, they reject the true God and live with a ruthless concern only for their own profit (see Psalm 10; Luke 12:13–21). But Israel's faith never allows money to become the true basis of trust or the basis of life itself (see Job 31:24; Ps 49:6 [7]). Those who are "fat" and "rich" (see Jer 5:26–28; Ps 73:4–12) are the opposite of the pious and upright. Another variant of idolatry is trust in political and military power. To oppose the monarchy, either during its ascendancy or even after its collapse, Israel recalled: "Yahweh will rule over you" (see Judg 8:23; Ps 8:1, 9 [2, 10]). Israel properly waits for Yahweh's help (see Isa 7:4; 30:15). Israel is admonished in worship not to "put your trust in princes" (Ps 146:3), thus calling to mind the lowly, through whom Yahweh makes known his power (Isa 52:13—53:12; note also the humiliation of Jesus and his followers as well as that of the earliest Christians: 1 Cor 1:26–28). In the Bible the political powerbrokers are normally seen as enemy—the Egyptian pharaoh, the apostate kings of Israel and Judah, the Roman governors, and the local vassals of the emperor. A fourth deviation from true worship is clerical autonomy. Like princes and kings, priests and prophets, too, can propagate false gods and lead the people astray (see Hos 4:4–6; Mic 3:5–8; Jer 5:31; 27–28; Ezekiel 13). Pharisees and Sadducees, the spiritual elite, become the bitter enemies of Jesus. In sum, the biblical message radically denounces every misuse of power by people who think themselves autonomous and equal to God and who thus practice false worship and encourage others to practice false worship.

Our problem is that patriarchal abuse of power—male arrogance at the expense of women—is virtually never addressed in the Bible. As we have seen, it is with a sense of lamentation that the woman in the older creation story is told: "He [the husband] shall rule over you" (Gen 3:16). According to everything we know about the Old Testament's critique of domination, this sentence can only mean that the priority of the male over the female helper is not the ideal situation and must finally be overcome. The somewhat mysterious text cited earlier (Jer 31:22) could mean to annul the curse on women and their dependence on men (see F. Crüsemann, 94ff.). Further, we can justifiably point to the liberating behavior of Jesus in regard to women, which called the Jewish tradition radically into question, and to the structures and forms of worship in the earliest Christian communities (and in many "heretical" groups) that were favorable to women. These came before the field became dominated by the claim that "women should be silent in churches" and are "saved through childbearing." But, finally, none of this is decisive. The Bible contains no direct call to free the slaves, and, similarly, no clear imperative regarding the emancipation of women. Why is this? One could name several historical realities, from chronic patriarchal blindness to the Christian community's imminent expectation of the end. In my opinion, it is essential to recognize that the discrimination against women in terms of their place in the larger society and exercise of alternative roles was simply not understood. Women and men lived and thought in terms of specific compartmentalized responsibilities within the common family. Problems, too, have their own "age of discovery," a fact that is often dramatically apparent today. Actions and attitudes that only a few years ago were seen as not at all problematic or threatening have become terrifying and monstrous—sometimes in a very short time. The intellectual roots for the contemporary debate about the emancipation of women lie in the Enlightenment. The external conditions for women's liberation have fully existed for only a few years. Countless women still have not made the change to a consciousness of emancipation. Feminist authors write with surprise, often deeply moved, about their own shift in consciousness. (This is found in many feminist works, from those of Mary Daly to Gerda Weiler.) All this shows very clearly how timely and time-conditioned the feminist awakening really is. This means that the women and men of the Bible could not have possessed this modern consciousness. Recognizing the historical difference between the way of life then and now means we need not dismiss the Bible as unimportant in these matters. To do so would be unwise, because the Bible's effects, especially in the area of discrimination, have been so strong. On the other hand, it is not necessary to retouch the biblical statements to match modern thought. That would be unwise, because such adjustments show themselves over time to be forced and intolerable. No, the fact that the emancipation of women is not an issue in the Bible invites us into dialogue with our spiritual ancestors. It does not hinder our putting questions to the biblical texts, even critical ones. Proceeding from our present problems, we are permitted to ask: How should we, here and now, respond to the criticisms and proposals of feminist theology? What can we say about the God who meets us today? (The point that this is finally the same God as the God of Abraham, Moses, and Jesus Christ is not particularly helpful, because all we can ever talk about are time-conditioned images of God, never "God himself.")

The primary difficulty in beginning this dialogue with our ancestors in faith is the indisputable fact, demonstrated in chapters 1 through 6, that the Old Testament and the whole Christian Bible do not present us with a single harmonious teaching about God, but rather with a variety of statements, each conditioned by time and social situation. Examining each of these statements shows that they are not simply transferable to our own situation. Therefore, we must seek in the Old Testament itself criteria for an understanding of God that transcend the passage of time and still have significance in our day. Consciously or unconsciously, every theology that works from ancient texts makes choices of this kind. In the process of interpretation the interpreter moves back and forth between the text and the present situation. It is important that the assumptions the interpreter carries along do not conceal the potential for the Bible's theological perspective to offer its own critique of the present. Theology dare not become a straitjacket for God—which, unfortunately, happens all too often. Some protection from the personal power of the interpreter— whether pastor or lay, man, woman, or child—is provided when all arguments are weighed critically against one another and the dialogue is carried out not only with the ancient texts, alone in the study, but also with living people, in the midst of their everyday experiences. I find the following four principles typical for the biblical images of God. They are also of decisive importance for our own time.

1. The biblical God is a personal God. The resemblance of the biblical God to the human, the obverse of the image of God in the human (Gen 1:26), has never been without its problems. God walks in the evening breeze of the garden of Eden (Gen 3:8); speaks with individual people, once even "face to face, as one speaks to a friend" (Exod 33:11); exhibits human emotions such as anger, remorse, and compassion; and acts with human incalcu-lability—all of which tend to confuse our theological thinking, which has been schooled in notions of philosophical abstraction. Nevertheless, it is good that the biblical traditions, despite all their attempts to present God's transcendence, have not sup-pressed these strongly anthropomorphic features that carry over from Israel's long prehistory. The God of the Bible is interested in people, which is the reason he is portrayed in human ways. The ultimate power is not some blind impenetrable fate but is avail-able for communication. That divine power creates and maintains not only the life of human beings but of the entire creation. Today we must emphatically insist on this latter point, a teaching found especially in the biblical material influenced by the wisdom tradi-tion, because our world is fundamentally threatened by human behavior.

This humane biblical deity is revealed in many forms, bears many names, and adapts to changes in human life and social struc-tures. As the Bible testifies again and again, at the center of God's concern is always the weal and woe of individual human beings within their own sphere of life, that is, within their small human communities. "I live among my own people," says the Shunam-mite woman to Elisha. She needs no word spoken on her behalf to higher authority (2 Kgs 4:13). The pictures of a quiet life under one's own vine and fig tree (see Mic 4:4) or of the peaceful life together in unity (Ps 133:1) express the religious expectations of the faithful. God fights for a good common life among human beings, since only in community can life be realized. Conflicts with neighbors, hostile groups, and conquerors demand resistance and self-defense, which unfortunately lead also to a desire for revenge and hegemony. Over and over again, the Israelites fell victim to the movements of peoples coursing through their land. Like all peoples, they fought for their own survival, calling their own God into this struggle. Greater and greater tribulation led during the exile to the doctrine of Israel's unique election and the corresponding subordination of all other peoples under the sole God Yahweh. (Earlier, in a time of Assyrian imperialistic expansion, that people had already proclaimed the worldwide rule of its god Assur.) In the Bible, God's dominion over the world is, however, never an end in itself. It serves to support the life of the "pious" and the "righteous" within the community of faith (see the late psalms, for example, Psalms 19; 37; 49; 119). So, even the broadest theological proposals, which presuppose a gathered people of Israel, maintain a concern for the elementary forms of human life. Under closer inspection, the Israelite nationalism of the Old Testament serves the good of the clans and communities. Images of divine sovereignty and splendor, of the subordination of the peoples and the final judgment on the last day (see Zeph 3:8; Matthew 25) are justified by the fact that they are imagined by suffering and oppressed people and intend to promote lives of human dignity (see Isa 65:17–25). The exclusion and destruction of other peoples or groups (see Isa 65:13–16) have only temporal or conditional character; they are never fundamental to the divine image (see Isa 19:16–25; 56:1–8).

The biblical God does distinguish between friend and enemy. That is as unavoidable in Israel's struggle for survival as it is in the present ongoing life and death struggles of the "third" and "fourth" world. But this God is no respecter of persons in assigning life-giving righteousness (see Ps 58:1 [2]; 82:1–4; Exod 23:1–9). Whether to poor or rich, native or stranger, the same rules of common life apply. Paul extends this principle in classic fashion: "There is no longer Jew or Greek, there is no longer slave or free, there is no longer male and female" (Gal 3:28). Before God, the deepest ethnic and social differences are of no importance. The biblical God is interested in humanity in all its various groupings. The forms of organized human society and the people within them are supported and corrected by God. The stress is traditionally on the small group, as befits the nature of Israel's relationship with God. Without question, the deity meets women and men with the same expectations and the same level of support. The Bible knows of no extended sexist theory or theology (see chapters 1 through 6). Movements that denigrate women are false directions within a biblical theology that is fundamentally open and self-critical. This is demonstrated in biblical tradition by, among other things, the fact that women have encounters with God and are God's partners in conversation (Genesis 16; Judges 13; 1 Samuel 1–2; Luke 1; Mark 16). As we claimed, the veneration of goddesses probably continued up into the time of the monarchy. In any case, prior to the exile women had their own legitimate participation in the Israelite cult.

2. The biblical God is transcendent and universal. God revealed himself to the ancient Israelites in his "humanity" and in no other way. But even this sentence recognizes God's otherness—a notion that remains attractive to us because of its testimony to God's perfection, even though we can explain or apprehend it so imperfectly. Actually, we should attempt to say nothing at all about the absolute God, just as the mystics were moved and filled with the divine, the sole beginning and end of all being, in eloquent silence. There is really nothing we can say about the deity in and of itself except that he/she/it is revealed in the concrete, in particular events. But we should and must point out some biblical vanishing lines that proceed from the concrete elements of individual experiences of faith and point beyond them, meeting at infinity. Just as a mysterious blueprint for life itself can be imagined and pieced together, albeit imperfectly, from the many different forms of life, just as the endless variety of stuff in the physical world finally points to a unity of material existence, so also we can imagine a distant and hidden unity in the temporally conditioned and ever-changing statements of faith and notions of God found in the Bible (and probably beyond the Bible in the testimonies of other religions).

The lines that point from individual biblical texts and individual acts of faith within our Judeo-Christian tradition toward the divine itself provide a perspective that protects us from succumbing in confusion to the many fleeting individual impressions; they give us the courage to avoid seeking God through continual navel-gazing or the destructive and complacent delusion that theology and church can arrive at absolute truth. God's perfection and inexplicability relativizes all images of God and all social relations, both past and present. It also relativizes every form of patriarchal theology and shows all sexist male theological fantasies, as well as all feminist theological models and counterproposals, to be temporally conditioned phenomena. It is only by knowing the relativity of all our attempts to do theology that we can freely think, discuss, and disagree, searching together for a truth for our own age. We can admit the incompleteness and the brevity of our own proposals; and despite our legitimate attempts to stake out honest positions, we will not need to condemn for all eternity those who disagree. God's transcendence and concomitant universality are necessary correlatives to God's humanness.

Human consciousness is mysteriously directed toward the eternal and the otherworldly; human hope seeks something permanent and fixed. Things were no different in Israel. In the Old Testament texts, people use their own instruments of imagination to find the otherworldly essence of the deity amid the various social and cultural contingencies. We will briefly examine this proposal to see how it applies to the concepts life, holiness, power, and permanence.

Yahweh is the "fountain of life" (Ps 36:9 [10]; cf. Jer 2:13; 17:13). He created life (Gen 2:19) and expressly breathed the breath of life into the human (Gen 2:7). All life is at Yahweh's disposal (see Hos 6:2; 2 Kgs 5:7; Deut 32:39). It is no wonder that he is called the "living God" (for example, 1 Sam 17:26; Jer 10:10; 23:36; Ps 42:3; 84:3). This title may contain echoes of a Canaanite-Mesopotamian festival of the rebirth of the dead fertility deity; but what is clear is that the God of the Bible (including the New Testament) is the owner and giver of life.

The "holiness" of an ancient oriental deity is the sphere of concentrated energy and light surrounding and proceeding from the deity; this field of energy both connects the deity to human beings and distances it from them. "Splendor," "brightness," "radiance," "glory," and similar terms are used in the Bible to describe holiness (see 1 Sam 6:20; Isa 6:3; Ps 63:2–4; 99:3; 104:1–2; Exod 24:16–17). The people of God and the whole earth participate in the blessings of God's holiness and splendor, but in careful doses (see Exod 19:5–6; Lev 19:2; Ps 65:9–13 [10–14]). Direct contact with the divine sphere produces instant death (see 2 Sam 6:6–7; Deut 5:24–26). In the early Christian church, it is still said that God "dwells in unapproachable light, whom no one has ever seen or can see" (1 Tim 6:16). We can best imagine what ancient people had in mind if we think of contemporary examples of concentrated energy, like the sun, combustion chambers in engines, radioactive material, explosives, or highly concentrated medications. Here too we have spheres of energy that are deadly in high concentration but life-giving in reasonable doses.

Similar characteristics are ascribed to Yahweh's "power," "might," "authority," and "strength." One might say that these terms portray the outward direction of God's holiness. This power is directed primarily against the enemies (see Ps 29; 68:28 [29]; 74:13; 89:11; Isa 59:16–17). The existence of evil in the world gives rise to Yahweh's use of power. Nevertheless, the Bible never fully defines the origin and essence of evil. Nor does it permit a dualistic split. Consequently, evil cannot be equated with the female or with any other generic phenomenon. Evil is experienced in chaos and the powers of death. To some degree, the human is at the mercy of evil (see Pss 73; 74; 77; 78).

Finally, the reservoir of God's powers of life never runs dry. It abides into the future, for Yahweh is a God in perpetuity. "Eternity" is not the proper term for what biblical theology means by *'olam* (see Isa 40:28; Pss 9:8; 66:7; 90:2; 92:8–9). But in human perspective the life of God endures forever. "For a thousand years in your sight are like yesterday when it is past" (Ps 90:4). This number may seem small to us when compared to Hindu and Buddhist notions of time or those of modern astronomy. But for the ancient Israelites the numbers 1,000 and 10,000 were regarded as immense and immeasurable. To Yahweh is attributed a stability and reliability that exceeds all human measure.

The concepts of "life," "holiness," "power," and "permanence," when related to Israel's God, betray a dynamic notion of the deity, a God who promotes and protects life. God has at his disposal an unending supply of beneficent powers, which are given in proper measure to the earth and to humanity. Though all of these terms derive from human experience, the basis for Yahweh's transcendence lies in his incomprehensibly abundant supply. With the growth of monotheism, this abundance gave rise also to God's universal significance for the entire human race. But does such thinking already contain the beginnings of a limitation of the deity to male concepts, for which many feminist theologians reproach the entire Old Testament tradition (see M. Daly; E. Sorge; G. Weiler)? Are the Bible's theological views, including even the unfathomable existence of God, corrupted by one-sidedly masculine patterns of thought?

As I see it, of the four areas just discussed, only power—and perhaps holiness—can be regarded as typically male images. "Life" and "permanence" are important to all humans, even though we rightly bemoan the missing female metaphors associated with creation and the nourishment of life. On the other hand, God's loving attention to humanity is described more in "female" behavior patterns and categories (see 3, below). No doubt we must honestly admit that the image of God in the Bible has been articulated primarily by men and is, therefore, in need of expansion. But that image was not deliberately given male form; there was no sexist or discriminatory intent. The deity is described in otherworldly and transcendent terms for the sake of both sexes and the whole human community. Female and extra-Israelite experiences of God have been included in the theology of the Old Testament.

In this connection, we must note again the reluctance of the biblical theologians to compare or identify God with anything human (Deut 4:15–18; 5:8–10). The Old Testament writers speak with dismay, joy, dread, or fear of God's superiority to things of this world, but they almost never try to penetrate this superiority. Conscious of their own limitations, they forgo projecting human differences, especially the difference between the sexes, onto the deity. This does not seem like a deliberate or absolute patriarchal orientation.

When Moses came down from the mountain, he brought with

him something of the splendor of the heavenly realm, producing fear among the people (Exod 34:29–30). The otherness of the transcendent God became visible, and with it the helplessness of those who were subject to this otherworldly brilliance. But the Israelite narrators face this dilemma not only with fear and dismay; they also address the insignificance of the human vis-à-vis the overwhelming power of God with humor:

> Moses said, "Show me your glory, I pray." And he [Yahweh] said, "I will make all my goodness pass before you, and will proclaim before you the name, 'The Lord'; and I will be gracious to whom I will be gracious, and will show mercy on whom I will show mercy. But," he said, "you cannot see my face; for no one shall see me and live." And the LORD continued, "See, there is a place by me where you shall stand on the rock; and while my glory passes by I will put you in a cleft of the rock, and I will cover you with my hand until I have passed by; then I will take away my hand, and you shall see my back; but my face shall not be seen." (Exod 33:18–23)

Disregarding textual problems and difficult questions of literary composition, the comedy is unmistakable: God stands next to Moses, covers Moses' eyes with his hand, and allows him a view of his backside. Even Moses, the greatest person in Israel's history of faith, is portrayed—with a wink—as an unsuspecting schoolboy. It is true that there are other, perhaps earlier, texts that speak more naturally about seeing God (Exod 24:9–11; Ps 17:15). But the development of the old story of Moses on Sinai in the Elijah narrative surely betrays later theological reflection:

> [The LORD] said, "Go out and stand on the mountain before the LORD, for the LORD is about to pass by." Now there was a great wind, so strong that it was splitting mountains and breaking rocks in pieces before the LORD, but the LORD was not in the wind; and after the wind an earthquake, but the LORD was not in the earthquake; and after the earthquake a fire, but the LORD was not in the fire; and after the fire a sound of sheer silence. When Elijah heard it, he wrapped his face in his mantle and went out and stood at the entrance of the cave. (1 Kgs 19:11–13)

The narrator wonders where and what kind of a God Yahweh is. He criticizes the common notion that powerful natural events prove God's appearance, including those described Exodus 19! Yahweh is not in the storm, earthquake, or fire. Instead, he speaks out of a comparatively insignificant event, calling the prophet to account. God exhibits his incomprehensible existence in the coin of everyday affairs.

3. The God of the Bible is a God of love. God is found among those who suffer. Christian reflection about appropriate images of God cannot divorce itself from its own postulates of faith—Jesus Christ and the New Testament. What does it mean for our understanding of God that we call ourselves Christian? What are the content and criteria for our search given in the life, speech, death, and resurrection of Jesus? What are the particular perspectives of the Christian church?

God did not first become human in Jesus. Through all the developments of Israel's history of faith, God was humane. But during the time of the Roman empire and Greco-Roman culture in Palestine, God's loving concern for humanity became concrete in an entirely new way in the particular form of Jesus of Nazareth. This is a fundamental fact for Christian men and women. As in the Old Testament, God's work begins with the proclamation of salvation to and the deliverance of the oppressed. Jesus comes to this world as a member of the lower class. In all his activity he gives preference to those who are rejected, sick, or lost. This is where early Christianity gets its indelible (though often betrayed) character of a religion of the underprivileged, as even Friedrich Nietzsche had to admit—much to his dismay. In Jesus, God shows himself once again as a "God of the little people."

Appropriate to the intellectual and religious climate of its day, the good news for the poor came clothed in apocalyptic forms and expectations. The expectation of the kingdom of God that would bring final justice to the distressed people of Israel had grown greater and greater since the Babylonian exile. This development may well have been influenced by Persian dualistic ideas about the coming end of the age and the decisive battle between good and evil. By the time of Jesus and in the years thereafter, the expectation had reached a fever pitch. New among Christians was the vibrant faith by which people thought they could recognize and begin already to celebrate the radical change of epochs. For Christians, truth itself, the very essence of things, no longer remained in the background or at a distance; it was no longer confined to a taboo zone that must be respected, a place in which people have no reason to be. God would soon show himself in all his truth and righteousness, love and liveliness. Apocalyptic means revelation. As Paul says, we will see "face to face" (1 Cor 13:12). The oppressive conditions of this world are irreparable; they must be overcome, radically and conclusively renewed. The "eager longing" of creation (Rom 8:19) can no longer be ignored. Creation, too, must be "set free from its bondage to decay" and "obtain the freedom of the glory of the children of God" (Rom 8:21). "For while we are still in this tent, we groan under our burden, because we wish not to be unclothed but to be further clothed, so that what is mortal may be swallowed up by life" (2 Cor 5:4). The first Christians looked for and expected an imminent transformation to immortality. This would fulfill the Old Testament promises:

> Indeed, to this very day, when they hear the reading of the old covenant, that same veil is still there, since only in Christ is it set aside. Indeed, to this very day whenever Moses is read, a veil lies over their minds; but when one turns to the LORD, the veil is removed. Now the LORD is the Spirit, and where the Spirit of the LORD is, there is freedom. And all of us, with unveiled faces, seeing the glory of the LORD as though reflected in a mirror, are being transformed into the same image from one degree of glory to another; for this comes from the LORD, the Spirit. (2 Cor 3:14–18)

In the century of Jesus' birth, this expectation of the end times formed the background for the revelation of God's love to human beings. God's love is anchored deep in the faith of the Old Testament. Yahweh and other earlier or contemporary deities had always cared for the oppressed, be they men, women, children, slaves, or foreigners. According to the tradition, the God of Israel accompanied the first human beings when they were expelled from paradise (Gen 3:21). God remains at the side of the one who murdered his brother (Gen 4:15). God sees to the survival of at least a few people at the time of the great flood (Gen 6:8; 7:1–8). God appears to Hagar, lost in the desert (Gen 16:7–11). He accompanies the patriarchs, Abraham, Isaac, and Jacob. God guides Joseph through serious temptation to the summit of power (Genesis 37–50). The examples can be multiplied: throughout the whole course of Israel's history Yahweh hears the cry of the needy (see Exod 2:24; 3:7; 6:5; 22:23, 27 [22, 26]; Deut 26:7; Judg 2:18; 1 Kgs 8:28–29; 2 Kgs 22:19; Ps 12:5 [6]); he identifies with their fate. The same thing can be discovered in the legal sections and the prophetic and worship books of the Old Testament. Only the wisdom literature seems occasionally to recommend resignation (Prov 29:13; Eccl 4:1–2). In the biblical witness, God is generally to be found on the side of the poor. This may be the theological result of Israel's suffering, experienced over the centuries by all levels of society.

The content of these theological notions of divine love and solidarity reflect human experience—how could they not?—especially the experience of small family groups, clans, and villages. The Hebrew terms for love and mercy include ideas of mutual responsibility, sacrifice, a sense of justice and human dignity, and respect for people, collectively and individually. We might say that the fundamental root of the biblical testimony to God's love was, from the beginning, the faith of the small group. But, as we have seen, this elementary faith was deeply influenced by female religiosity. Because of their domestic responsibilities, women were always decisively important and determinative for the internal life of the community. If one can speak historically at all of a specific female contribution to our understanding of God, then this would be the place. The household gods of fertility and blessing were presumably also the protectors of internal family community, solidarity, and love. That the weaker members of society (in comparison to the stronger male leaders)—that is, the sick and aged, children, slaves, and women—were, on the other hand, often victimized (see Ps 71) is a part of the structural injustice that often went unnoticed in that historical context. In our day, however, this is quite another matter.

It may seem strange that I do not speak here of the God of

order and punishment. This God is, of course, massively present in the biblical writings. To some degree, discipline, correction, jealousy, and punishment are even integrated into God's solidarity with his people. In another place, I, too, would acknowledge the validity of a theology of order. But in today's world the prevailing hierarchical, imperialistic, economic, cultural, ethnic, and patriarchal systems of order are so fundamentally outmoded that Christian theology can no longer accept them as given points of departure. Therefore, male and female theologians who are trying to think in other than traditional ways rightly begin with God's dynamic and transforming love.

4. The biblical God is a liberating God. It is not sufficient to adhere to God's empathy with the weak as the sole theological axiom in our understanding of God. In our society, which is hypnotically fixed on securing the existing systems of power, we must state emphatically that the biblical God demanded, more than once, the removal of injustice. Naturally there were instances in which God stepped in to support the existing systems of government (see 2 Samuel 7; Psalm 2) or in which people appealed to him to restore such imperial order (see Psalm 89). Alongside this political order, the Old Testament is, of course, also concerned with the spiritual order of a world that was sinking in sin and impurity, an order that could be maintained only by daily priestly ritual sacrifices (cf. Leviticus 19; Num 28:1–8). (These sacrifices were, to be sure, sometimes strongly attacked and challenged even in that day; cf. Amos 5:21–24; Ps 50; and so on.) But, in my opinion, in the present situation, in which the world is weighed down with oppressive injustice and violence, with contempt for both humanity and God, we must reach back to the radically liberating and transforming traditions of the Bible and apply them to our own time.

The "liberating" traditions of the Bible have been rediscovered in the "third" world, above all in Latin America. The exodus of the Hebrew slaves (Exodus 1–15) is the great paradigm from Israel's early history. The stories of deliverance from the premonarchic period belong in the same category (for example, Judg 4–5; 7; 11; 13–16; 1 Samuel 11; 13). Yahweh frees his people by means of commanders anointed by the Spirit. Women play a decisive

role in these primeval events that establish Israel's identity. The
end of Babylonian dominance is also celebrated as an act of liberation (see Isa 43:14–21; 48:20–21; 51:11; 52:4–6). In liturgical
texts for worship (the Psalms), the liberation of the people is a
resounding theme (succinctly in Ps 66:12: "we went through fire
and through water; yet you have brought us out to a spacious
place"; see Psalms 68; 105; 136). In addition, we have the more
primal witness in the thanksgivings of those who have been delivered from everyday afflictions like illness, hunger, false accusation, ensnarement by guilt, or contempt by others. Their personal
God has brought them to "a broad place" (Ps 31:8 [9]), snatched
them from the jaws of hell or the pit of the underworld (see Ps
30:1, 3 [2, 4]; 40:2 [3]; 116:8). It is astonishing how fully the Old
Testament lawgivers are engaged with the plight of the miserable.
The actual laws, like those in comparable ancient Near Eastern
law codes, provide for a certain protection of underprivileged persons. But the hortatory and explanatory additions to the laws, that
derive no doubt from Israel's worship life, speak of the active intervention of God for the weak (cf. Exod 22:21–24 [20–23]; Deuteronomy 15; Leviticus 25). The problem of the marginal groups
is taken up often with the example of slaves, widows and orphans,
the handicapped, and the resident aliens (see also Jeremiah 34;
Nehemiah 5; Lev 19:9–10; 14–15; 33–34). The theologians of that
era fought actively for the removal of structural inequalities because they knew there is a God who recognizes the equality of all
families and who tolerates no class distinctions. They come close
to producing a social theory: "There will . . . be no one in need
among you" (Deut 15:4). "No one shall rule over the other
with harshness" (Lev 25:46). Each of these principles of equality
is based in theology, in the image of God. Yahweh, or a pre-
Yahwistic deity, commands solidarity with the neighbor and active intervention on his or her behalf. The deity is not content
with the existing order, the state of human relations; indeed, with
the whole system of values. He demands change, the overthrow of
dehumanizing systems, liberation from coerced domination. This
tendency sometimes influences even the usually conservative wisdom tradition, in which people are urged to rescue "those taken
away to death" (Prov 24:11). As everyone knows, it energizes the

prophetic voices throughout the Bible. From Amos and Hosea to Isaiah, Micah, and Jeremiah, to the postexilic prophetic preachers (see Isaiah 56; 58; Zechariah 7), we find numerous attacks on the established mechanisms of exploitation and on the rapacious elite (including clerics), in favor of the downtrodden in Israel and the whole world. Thus, "liberation" has rightly been rediscovered as a central biblical theme (see Isa 61:1–3 and Luke 4:16–19). For "the wretched of the earth" (F. Fanon) it is the very center of Christian theology. The rich industrialized nations of the northern hemisphere must turn around and make this their concern as well if the earth is not to be destroyed by their megalomania (cf. A. Tevoedjre).

Once again, control questions are indispensable to our investigation. Have I retained a patriarchal orientation in the four criteria I have defined for a biblical understanding of God today? Is my attempt to extend the Bible's theological approaches into our own time even possible? And, the most important question about God, does he (or she) still play the role of liberator in the very different social structures of our own day, that is, among those exploited by the world economy, among threatened ethnic and religious minorities, and especially among women? For my part, I want to answer these questions decisively in favor of the biblical (Old Testament) understanding of God. The image of God given in the Judeo-Christian tradition and continuing in our culture and faith is not yet ready to be retired. But an essential presupposition for doing biblical theology is a basic recognition of the way things really are in church and theology. This was the case in biblical times as well. Without an analysis and critique of the times, biblical theology was and is impossible. Today, this analysis must also include careful attention to and adoption of the feminist critique of God. Such an undertaking, examining all the pros and cons, would easily fill many books. In closing, I will limit myself to a series of summary theses and questions meant to incorporate more fully the difficulties facing theology today.

1. We are people living on the verge of the third millennium c.e. We experience and are shaped by the world in its present sociopolitical state. We interpret the world with today's conventional empirical and intellectual means and models, developed

since the Enlightenment and under the influence of the natural sciences. Recent history has brought the human race together with increasing speed. An important consequence is that our theology needs to have a global or universal goal, that is, it must keep in mind the fate of the whole earth and of all people. We know only too well that any individual theologian, male or female, or any individual congregation or ecclesiastical community, can offer only a limited perspective on the whole. Regional, cultural, class, and other limitations seriously impede our universality. The prospect of a global theology produced by limited and anything but universal human beings offers great opportunity for modesty and mutual understanding.

2. Theology is always concerned with the foundation and meaning of the whole world, with all its creatures and circumstances, conditions and connections. Theology is particularly related to life—without, however, excluding inanimate nature, the foundation of all life. Christian theology is oriented above all toward the tradition received, lived, and founded anew by Jesus of Nazareth. This tradition places at its center the one God, who is love, justice, and hope, and, alongside this God, human beings, without regard for sex, race, or confession. Christian faith has always held firmly to the unity of the world, contradicting, for the sake of humanity, every dualistic separation of the world into mutually exclusive realms (though there have also always been dualistic models of belief both within and without the "official" religion). Nevertheless, Christians have actively and passively opposed evil, also for the sake of the neighbor. The mainstream of Christian tradition has battled suffering, cross, and death as powers opposed to God, powers that were, at the same time, annulled by God's universal decree. Will feminist theology and women's experience open new dimensions of unity for the world? On the other hand, do some models of emancipation and liberation amount to new (old) ontological dualisms? Can a theory of fully autonomous individuality ever produce mutuality?

3. Humanity's millennia-old habit of thinking in terms of dominion, hegemony, and competition is today endangering the survival of the planet earth. Every year it costs the lives of several million creatures, human beings included. Christian faith and the

Christian image of God dare no longer be misused to legitimize domination and exploitation. Biblical principles of equality and modern declarations of human rights are binding for Christian theology. We need to seek more intensively ways to recognize the causes of human megalomania. Historically, dominant behavior has certainly been exercised more by men; for millennia, men were the overseers of the community's external affairs, learning in the process to meet danger with aggression and to consolidate their own positions through the use of power. But women, too, are not immune to the lure of exercising dominion over others. How can all of us together, from the lowest to the highest, dismantle our lust for domination or transform it into a willingness to serve?

4. Every creature needs appropriate access to the deity. Many biblical passages, as well as the painters of medieval altarpieces, expressly include even animals in this claim. But will the claim to such access mean that every community, every class, every race, each gender has to define its own God or have its own patron deity? Or can the one deity be all in all? At the very least, barriers between human beings and God defined by things such as privilege, ordination, or sexism, must be eliminated. Every person is directly related to God and no one dare use role stereotypes to deny another her or his full religious development. This applies also to the admission to ministerial offices in the various religious communities. Present principles of equality exclude discrimination just as fully as do the basic tendencies of the various biblical traditions. Nevertheless, must we not hold on to the unity of God while allowing variable images? Just as regional peculiarities show up in our theologies, the way we speak of God may differ among different individuals, congregations, stations, and classes. These different images of God, however, must all be related to and make known the global Whole—which means that individual theologies must remain in mutual conversation. They dare not make their own isolated truth claims. Only in dialogue with one another will they arrive at proper faith and true knowledge of God. Female deities alongside male ones, proletarian gods among capitalistic ones, black gods along with white ones, will only absolutize the class and race structures of our world.

5. "God is love, and those who abide in love abide in God, and God abides in them" (1 John 4:16). How does God's love relate to the use and application of power and force? What distinguishes love as the basic energy of the world from erotic love—or what connects them? In the first place, love may require a person to fight, even with a weapon. At least that is the argument of the German commission called to evaluate those claiming conscientious objection to military service. But it is also the argument of many Christian base communities in Latin America. Militant love is their slogan. Does there have to be a place for militant love along with self-giving love, the love that includes and harmonizes all things? As long as conflict and opposition remain, militant love will be necessary. But it must stay love. The use of force dare occur only in the context of an overarching solidarity. As a rule, militant love will limit itself to nonviolent, passive resistance and the inner transformation of suffering and injustice.

What about the connection to erotic love? Almost universally, Christianity has seen erotic love as a dubious and disturbing reality. The result has been hostility to the body, prudery, and various neurotic repressions and inhibitions. In the Old Testament, on the other hand, we found an astonishingly unabashed use of love metaphors for the relationship between God and people. It is certainly time for the Judeo-Christian tradition to overcome the subliminal and dualistic separation between the physical or sensual and the "higher" spiritual (and male) reality. In a male-oriented society, every suppression of the erotic necessarily leads to the denigration of women. Thus, the inclusion of all forms of love in our understanding of God is urgently required. This does not deny the fact that there are perversions and abuses of love. But a God who is the source of life certainly has a place for eros.

6. Our world, divided by deadly antitheses, requires a comprehensive change in its consciousness and social structures. The survival of the human race and the ongoing existence of life itself is at stake. The liberation suggested by biblical theology and demanded by contemporary experience concerns all human beings and all of life. Year after year, numerous plant and animal species are destroyed forever. In many places native populations are threatened with eradication by the greedy advance of "civiliza-

tion." (Examples include the Yamomami Indians in Brazil and the Aborigines in Australia.) The slippery slope of economic exploitation euphemistically called the North-South conflict holds more than half the world's population in dehumanizing dependence. People are starving daily in the southern hemisphere, or they are forced to live in the garbage dumps of the rich or from crime and prostitution. Antagonism between classes and races cuts through every society. The exploitation and degradation of women crosses every previously mentioned division. More than a century ago, August Bebel saw the emancipation of women as an essential part of the "social problem." Until women reach equality in public life, none of humanity's problems can be considered solved. But the opposite is also true: the whole latticework of economic, political, and racial oppression must always be kept in view during a discussion of feminist concerns. Otherwise a justified desire for emancipation could inadvertently contribute to new structures of oppression or strengthen the old ones. We are in search of a theology that brings justice, peace, and love to all people.

Biblical Exegesis and Biblical Theology in the Light of Feminist Critique

The consensus among biblical scholars that was said to exist in the 1950s and 1960s has given way to a diversity of theological opinions. Increasingly, our basic hermeneutical rules, exegetical insights, and biblical theologies have been called into question, especially by the countries of the "third" and "fourth" worlds; by thoughtful contemporaries concerned for human rights, the politics of peace, and the survival of the environment; and by feminist theologians of both sexes. All these challenges have one thing in common: they put the foundations of our traditional biblical faith to the test. Therein lies a threat to the existing ecclesiastical and social structures but also an opportunity for the radical evangelical renewal of our life.

In what follows I will consider only a few of the challenges from feminist theology; I see all of these within the framework of the global changes indicated above.

1. Feminist criticism is kindled by the patriarchal realities that continue to prevail: despite advances made by women in leadership roles at lower levels, now as always men play the dominant roles in church and society. In retrospect, the Judeo-Christian tradition has come to be recognized as more or less inimical to women. And, despite a few emancipating passages, the roots of this discrimination lie in the normative biblical texts and the predominantly patriarchal images of God they present.

In response, speaking from an exegetical perspective, let me say the following:

1.1 The criticism of patriarchy is, on the whole, justified. In the Judeo-Christian tradition, women have, as a rule, borne the brunt of the work and often enough the additional burden of being regarded as religiously suspect, perhaps even heretical. Even today, women are largely excluded from participation in the highest decision-making councils. Male pride has often sought to gain status by portraying women negatively. The church, still predominantly ruled by men, and the theological schools, defined by men, have every reason to do penance and admit their failures.

1.2 There is only muted criticism of patriarchal structures in the Bible and very little in the church. "Patriarchy" could be fundamentally challenged only after the Enlightenment had raised the individual, with his or her naturally bestowed dignity and inalienable rights, to the top of the scale of ethical values. Previously held corporate ways of thinking faded into the background. It follows from this historical perspective that we cannot simply project today's criteria for human emancipation back into the Judeo-Christian tradition. The preeminent status of the individual in its modern form was unknown to the biblical writers.

1.3 Thus, the biblical texts are to be interpreted in the light of their historical background. Without doubt, patriarchal conditions prevailed throughout the entire ancient Near East. Women, children, and slaves were subject to the head of the family. Nevertheless, the extended family or clan understood itself as an organic whole in which every member had to accept traditionally assigned functions and to practice solidarity with the others. Even the patriarchal leader was subject to the norms and constraints of the group and could not capriciously exploit other members of the group for his own egoistic motives (see Genesis 38, especially v. 26).

1.4 In human terms, the patriarchal God Yahweh, as encountered in Israel's exclusive monotheistic confession since the time of the exile (see Second Isaiah), is a reflection of the father figure known in Israelite society. Yahweh was called King, LORD, and Father; he demonstrated solidarity with his people (see Hos 11:1–9; Ps 103:6–13). Yahweh returns honor and prosperity to a defeated, plundered, and abused people by making them once more his family in a new covenant (see Isaiah 60–62; Jeremiah 30–31; Ezekiel 36–37). With such a cooperative understanding of patriarchy in the exilic/postexilic period, the female element was still able to find a place in the divine image (see Isa 66:13—"As a mother comforts her child, so I will comfort you").

1.5 Recent studies have made increasingly clear that there was no antifemale discrimination in the expressions of faith of pre-exilic Israel (see U. Winter; O. Keel, *Monotheismus*). We recognize there a pragmatic patriarchalism based on an equal distribution of functions between the sexes within the economic unit of the extended family. Women probably enjoyed their own uncontested religious and cultic sphere (see Gen 31:19, 34; Jer 44:17–19), and "Yahweh and his Asherah" were worshiped in many of the rural temples (see the discussion in chapter 3).

1.6 Female cultic practices and the worship of goddesses came to be suppressed only as part of Israel's concentration on a single exclusive God and its separation from all foreign cultures in the exilic/postexilic period. Even in priestly circles, discrimination against female religious expression could not arise until that time. On the basis of ancient taboos against the mixing of two sub-stances (Deut 22:19–29) or two spheres of power, the priests had to keep the cultic life free of every female influence (see Lev 18:19–29; and, earlier, 1 Sam 21:4–6 [5–7]). The exclusion of women from the cult of Yahweh, which was reserved for men, and the simultaneous prohibition of all other cultic activity meant that the female cults could continue only by going underground. There they continued to be a danger to the official priestly cult. Women's religiosity was branded as inimical to God and of lesser value (see 1 Sam 28; Jer 44:15–19.), and the woman was labeled a sexual and religious temptress (Eve; Jezebel).

1.7 The prohibition of images (Exod 20:4–6; cf. Deut 4:16) shows that, at the same time, Israel's theologians were fully aware of God's transcendence. Yahweh had no form that could be iden-tified with any being in the world of human experience. He was seen especially to transcend sexual differentiation (Deut 4:16). Though there were de facto discriminatory practices against women (exclusion from the priesthood, purity laws, dissolution of "mixed marriages"), these were not given theological basis in the Old Testament. That move is made in the New Testament with the appeal to the orders of creation (see 1 Cor 11:2–16; 14:34–35;

Eph 5:22–24). Nevertheless, God's nature is never expressly defined in sexually specific terms.

1.8 In evaluating Israel's history of faith with regard to the present discussion, we must resolutely begin our theological reflections with the intervening changes in social and ethnic conditions. The patriarchal structures and concepts that were in force prior to the Enlightenment have now been partially overcome in the areas of economics, education, and culture; often, in declarations of fundamental rights, legislation, and legal practice, they have been effectively disestablished. Patriarchal thought patterns are theoretically antiquated, though, to be sure, still operative in daily life. The proclamation of the compassionate and liberating God of the Bible must take into account the present situation. Today, bringing liberation to the humanity intended by creation will include the emancipation of the economically exploited majority of the world's population as well as full equal rights for people of color and for women.

2. Both male and female feminist theologians often support their critique of patriarchy by appealing to J. J. Bachofen's matriarchal hypothesis. In this view, the great earth-, moon-, and mother-goddess was the primary deity of prehistorical and early historical times. Corresponding to this priority of the goddess, women set the tone for human society, giving life a female orientation. Men were allotted merely serving roles, both in heaven and on earth (cf. H. Göttner-Abendroth). Under this female leadership, a condition of peace, harmony, and good fortune prevailed until male aggressiveness brought an end to this nearly paradisiacal situation.

In response, let me note the following, from the perspective of the exegete.

2.1 Ascribing specifically feminine characteristics to women has a long tradition, from Aristotle to Jung and beyond. Women's nature is said to be marked above all by passivity and emotion. Occasionally, womanliness is described as a separate category of being and, as such, anchored in metaphysics. No such speculations can be found in the literatures of the ancient Near East. In fact, Judith Ochshorn clearly documents ancient Near Eastern notions whereby "female" characteristics (for example, ability to love, fertility) and "male" attributes (for example, strength of will, brutality) were in no way distributed according to gender in the myths of those cultures but instead were equally ascribed to both gods and goddesses.

2.2 One often finds in feminist theologies an idealistic elevation of allegedly female natural characteristics. Female nature and female spirituality are seen as life-enhancing and good while male nature and male striving incline toward evil and death. Such a dualistic division of human nature will not stand up to psychological and empirical testing (see M. Mitscherlich; S. Heine), nor is it theologically tenable. Despite all the role differentiation between the sexes, the Bible sees human nature as undivided (see F. Gaiser). Even the priests, with all their penchant for dividing and delimiting, hold male and female together in one species (Gen 1:27). People of both sexes are included in both the accusations and promises of the Bible, very often not as individuals but in social groupings.

2.3 The comprehensive matriarchal hypothesis (matriarchy = paradise; patriarchy = fall and misery) is not historically demonstrable, though there were and are societies in which women exercise more public power and responsibility than in the patriarchally structured ancient Near East. Where a patriarchal organization of society is pragmatic and functional rather than ontological, women can, in particular situations, assume male functions (in the Bible, for example, Deborah, Jael, Abigail, Hulda, Athaliah, and the Shunammite woman). The general rule, verifiable by ethnology, is that, as a consequence of the distribution of labor within the economic unit of the family, the man assumed external responsibilities (hunting, war, cultivation of the fields, breeding livestock) and the woman the domestic tasks (child care, cooking, garden, domestic animals); this has probably been true since the beginnings of human history (see S. de Beauvoir).

2.4 Biblical religion and the other religions in the ancient Near East take account of female identity and visibly validate it in goddess worship or by giving female characteristics to the patriarchal god. Biblical texts permit the assumption that, before the collapse of 587 B.C.E., Israel permitted the cult of the goddess both in the household and at designated temples. This is confirmed by the discovery of numerous portrayals of the naked goddess in Israelite cities from the monarchic period (cf. U. Winter). Old Testament personal names demonstrate that there were dedicated female followers of Yahweh (see Jochebed, in Exod 6:20; Noadiah, in Neh 6:14). The worship of god/goddess pairs was apparently widespread in the ancient Near East among both men and women. All of this speaks for the recognition of gender-specific religious expression, but against a dualistic division of the faith.

2.5 Today's burning theological question is how, given our changed social conditions, contemporary imaging of God can accommodate the legitimate desire for the positive expression of women's reality. Since a patriarchal notion of God no longer corresponds to the way we seek to structure life, theological affirmations must include both female and male individuality and be open to both sexes (not to mention finding ways to bridge racial, national, ideological, and social antitheses). To be concrete, I see four possibilities.

2.5.1 We replace the exclusively male understanding of God with one that is exclusively female ("Back to the goddess"). However, merely reversing patriarchal forms of dominion would hardly be fully renewing and liberating.

2.5.2 We make an earnest attempt to understand the one God of the late Old Testament, of the New Testament, and of all Judeo-Christian people equally as mother and father, father and mother. God, previously seen in almost exclusively male terms, then becomes an androgynous being. This way of overcoming one-sided patriarchal thinking is quite far advanced in the United States. Even in worship, God is most often addressed as a "He/She" person.

2.5.3 Alternatively, we could call upon a female God alongside the male God. The difficulty with this is that, especially in Protestant tradition, there is no way to accommodate the ancient worship of divine pairs. As things stand now, a bifurcation of God would probably also result in a divided church.

2.5.4 In my opinion, the most promising way to overcome the male usurpation of the divine image is consistently to employ gender-neutral metaphors. There have been many models for this kind of God-talk since Near Eastern antiquity. In the Old Testament, God is related to wind, spirit, light, fire, goodness, breadth, forgiveness, and so on. Since then, many other gender-neutral associations have been used. We can do without a vocabulary that implies domination or one that is gender-specific in the traditional way.

2.6 A rethinking of theology's center, its talk to and about God, must take into account the concerns of women. Such new thinking will naturally have consequences for the way the sexes live together in family, society, and church. All forms of congregational life (worship, working groups, other associations) must be just as completely rethought and reconstituted as are theology and doctrine, church governance and administrative structures.

3. The ongoing discussion about the foundations and goals of our faith involves many areas (world economy, ecumenicity, views of the human, politics of peace). It is often very vigorous. The necessary conversation with feminist theologies is no exception. It is one of the debates within the church that will have profound consequences. What is needed is an objective conversation appropriate to the seriousness of the issue, a conversation in which all participants, women and men, are willing to listen to one another, to make adjustments in their own position, and, with responsibility to both the past and the future, to search constructively for common solutions.

3.1 These common solutions must be the goal of theological reflection. In a time when extreme individualism appears to be a basic principle of life, Christians, with the help of the God who desires the unity and harmony of creation, can seek new forms of common life. In many places, the Bible contains a revolutionary criticism of authority (see Judges 9; Isaiah 52–53; Luke 1–2; John 13). The intention is clear: the protection of life, dignity, and human rights, especially of the weak. Referring to bond-servants, Lev 25:43 says, "You shall not rule over them with harshness, but shall fear your God." The biblical message centers on the liberation of all people, and this must remain our guiding principle as well. But in the biblical view, the presupposition and goal of human liberation is communal—a community free of domination.

3.2 All of our contemporary theological conversations require both openness and passion. However, we must also seek criteria appropriate to finding truth. On the one hand, as in all exegesis,

the discussion takes place among the various partners in the contemporary conversation. The individual participants in that conversation must carefully and self-critically clarify their own positions; they must analyze the contemporary situation to arrive at
conclusions about the degree of enslavement of human groups
and classes, about secular liberation movements, about the function and reformability of existing structures. But, on the other
hand, the dialogue must also include our biblical mothers and fathers. That is the only conversation that can protect us from dead
ends and false directions. Freed of its patriarchal moorings, the
promise given to the city of Jerusalem can serve as our guide:

> No more shall the sound of weeping be heard in it, or the cry of dis-
> tress. No more shall there be in it an infant that lives but a few days,
> or an old person who does not live out a lifetime; for one who dies at
> a hundred years will be considered a youth, and one who falls short of
> a hundred will be considered accursed. (Isa 65:19–20)

> For I am about to create new heavens and a new earth; the former
> things shall not be remembered or come to mind. (Isa 65:17)

Bibliography

Albertz, Rainer. *A History of Israelite Religion in the Old Testament Period.* 2 vols. Translated by John Bowden. Louisville, Ky.: Westminster John Knox Press, 1994.

———. *Persönliche Frömmigkeit und offizielle Religion: Religionsinterner Pluralismus in Israel und Babylon.* Stuttgart: Calwer Verlag, 1978.

Alt, Albrecht. "The God of the Fathers." In *Essays on Old Testament History and Religion.* Translated by R. A. Wilson, 1–100. Garden City, N.Y.: Doubleday, 1967.

Asher-Greve, Julia M. *Frauen in altsumerischer Zeit.* Malibu, Calif.: Undena, 1985.

Bachofen, J. J. *Myth, Religion, and Mother Right.* Translated by Ralph Manheim. Princeton: Princeton University Press, 1967.

Badinter, Elisabeth. *Man/Woman: The One Is the Other.* Translated by Barbara Wright. London: Collins Harvill, 1989.

de Beauvoir, Simone. *The Second Sex.* Translated and edited by H. M. Parshley. New York: Alfred A. Knopf, 1952.

Bebel, August. *Woman and Socialism.* Translated by Meta L. Stern. New York: Socialist Literature Co., 1910.

Becker-Schmidt, Regina, and Gudrun Knapp. *Geschlechtertrennung—Geschlechterdifferenz.* 2nd ed. Bonn: Dietz, 1989.

Beyerlin, Walter, ed. *Religionsgeschichtliches Textbuch zum Alten Testament.* Göttingen: Vandenhoeck & Ruprecht, 1975.

Borneman, Ernest. *Das Patriarchat.* 8th ed. Frankfurt: Fischer, 1991.

Brenner, Athalya. "Female Social Behavior: Two Descriptive Patterns within the 'Birth of Hero' Paradigm." *Vetus Testamentum* 36 (1986): 257–273.

Brunner-Traut, Emma. *Die alten Ägypter: Verborgenes Leben unter Pharaonen.* 4th ed. Stuttgart: Kohlhammer, 1987.

Burkert, Walter. *Homo Necans: The Anthropology of Ancient Greek Sacrificial Ritual and Myth.* Translated by Peter Bing. Berkeley, Calif.: University of California Press, 1983.

Burns, Rita. *Has the* Lord *Indeed Spoken Only through Moses? A Study of the Biblical Portrait of Miriam.* Atlanta: Scholars Press, 1987.

Cross, Frank M. "Yahweh and the Gods of the Patriarchs." *Harvard Theological Review* 55 (1962): 225–259.

Crüsemann, Frank. "'. . . er aber soll dein Herr sein' (Genesis 3:16)." In Frank Crüsemann and Hartwig Thyen, *Als Mann und Frau geschaffen: Exegetische Studien zur Rolle der Frau.* Gelnhausen/Berlin: Burckhardthaus-Verlag, 1978.

Daly, Mary. *Beyond God the Father: Toward a Philosophy of Women's Liberation.* Boston: Beacon Press, 1973.

———. *The Church and the Second Sex.* New York: Harper & Row, 1968.

———. *Gyn/ecology: The Metaethics of Radical Feminism.* Boston: Beacon Press, 1978.

Day, John. "Asherah," in *The Anchor Bible Dictionary*, vol. 1, ed. David Noel Freedman. 483–487. New York: Doubleday, 1992.

Durkheim, Emile. *The Elementary Forms of the Religious Life.* Translated by Joseph Ward Swain. New York: Free Press, 1965 [1912].

Emerton, J. A. "New Light on Israelite Religion: The Implications of the Inscriptions from Kuntillet 'Ajrud." *Zeitschrift für die Alttestamentliche Wissenschaft* 94/1 (1982): 2–20.

Fanon, Frantz. *The Wretched of the Earth.* Translated by Constance Farrington. New York: Grove Press, 1963.

Firestone, Shulamith. *The Dialectic of Sex: The Case for Feminist Revolution.* New York: Morrow, 1970.

Friedan, Betty. *The Feminine Mystique.* 20th anniversary ed. New York: W. W. Norton, 1983.

Frymer-Kensky, Tikva. *In the Wake of the Goddesses: Women, Culture, and the Biblical Transformation of Pagan Myth.* New York: Free Press, 1992.

Gaiser, Frederick J. "Flying Bumblebees, Christian Feminists, and Other Impossible Possibilities." *Word & World* 15/3 (1995): 342–348.

Galling, Kurt. *Textbuch zur Geschichte Israels.* 2nd ed. Tübingen: J. C. B. Mohr, 1968.

Gerstenberger, Erhard S., and Wolfgang Schrage. *Woman and Man.* Translated by Douglas W. Stott. Nashville: Abingdon, 1981.

Gibson, John C. L. *Textbook of Syrian Semitic Inscriptions*, vol. 1: *Hebrew and Moabite Inscriptions.* Oxford: Clarendon Press, 1971.

Glennon, Lynda M. *Woman and Dualism: A Sociology of Knowledge Analysis.* New York: Longman, 1979.

Göttner-Abendroth, Heide. *Die Göttin und ihr Heros.* 6th ed. Munich: Frauenoffensive, 1984.

Haag, Ernst, ed. *Gott, der einzige: Zur Entstehung des Monotheismus in Israel.* Freiburg: Herder, 1985.

Halkes, Catharina J. M. *Suchen was verlorenging: Beiträge zur feministischen Theologie.* Gütersloh: Gütersloher Verlag, 1985.

Hebblethwaite, Margaret. *Motherhood and God.* London: G. Chapman, 1984.

Heine, Susanne. "Female Masochism and the Theology of the Cross." *Word & World* 15/3 (1995): 299–305.

Hinkelammert, Franz J. *The Ideological Weapons of Death: A Theological Critique of Capitalism.* Translated by Philip Berryman. Maryknoll, N.Y.: Orbis Books, 1986.

Hite, Shere. *Woman and Love: A Cultural Revolution in Progress.* New York: Alfred A. Knopf, 1987.

Hyatt, J. Philip. *Commentary on Exodus.* New Century Bible. London: Oliphants, 1971.

Illich, Ivan. *Gender.* New York: Pantheon Books, 1982.

Jeremias, Joachim. "Abba." In *Abba: Studien zur neutestamentlichen Theologie und Zeitgeschichte,* 15–67. Göttingen: Vandenhoeck & Ruprecht, 1966.

Jeremias, Jörg. *Theophanie.* 2nd ed. Neukirchen-Vluyn: Neukirchener Verlag, 1977.

Keel, Othmar. *The Symbolism of the Biblical World: Ancient Near Eastern Iconography and the Book of Psalms.* New York: Seabury, 1978.

————, ed. *Monotheismus im Alten Israel und seiner Umwelt.* Fribourg: Verlag Schweizerisches Katholisches Bibelwerk, 1980.

Kirchenkanzlei der Evangelische Kirche in Deutschland. *Die Frau in Familie, Kirche, und Gesellschaft: Eine Studie zum gemeinsamen Leben von Frau and Man.* 2nd ed. Gütersloh: Gütersloher Verlagshaus Gerd Mohn, 1980.

Kluckhohn, Clyde, and Dorothea Leighton. *The Navaho.* Rev. ed. Revisions by Lucy Wales and Richard Kluckhohn. Cambridge, Mass.: Harvard University Press, 1974.

Kraus, Hans-Joachim. *Psalms 60–150: A Commentary.* Minneapolis: Augsburg Press, 1989.

Lang, Bernhard, ed. *Der einzige Gott: Die Geburt des biblischen Monotheismus.* Munich: Kösel, 1981.

Leipoldt, Johannes. *Die Frau in der antiken Welt und im Urchristentum.* Gütersloh: Gerd Mohn, 1962.

Lemaire, André, "Who or What Was Yahweh's Asherah?" *Biblical Archaeology Review* 10/6 (November/December 1984): 42–51.

Lewenhak, Sheila. *Women and Work.* New York: St. Martin's Press, 1980.

Loth, Heinrich. *Woman in Ancient Africa.* Translated by Sheila Marnie. Westport, Conn.: L. Hill & Co., 1987.

Mead, Margaret. *Male and Female: A Study of the Sexes in a Changing World.* New York: Morrow, 1949.

Menzel, Brigitte. *Assyrische Tempel.* 2 vols. Rome: Biblical Institute Press, 1981.

Meshel, Ze'ev. "Did Yahweh Have a Consort?" *Biblical Archaeology Review* 5/2 (March/April 1979): 24–35.

Meyers, Carol L. "Gender Roles and Genesis 3:16 Revisited." In Carol Meyers, ed., *The Word of the* LORD *Shall Go Forth: Essays in Honor of David Noel Freedman,* 337–354. Winona Lake, In.: Eisenbruns, 1983.

Mitscherlich, Alexander. *Society without the Father: A Contribution to Social Psychology.* Translated by Eric Mosbacher. New York: Schocken Books, 1970.

Mitscherlich, Margarete. *The Peaceable Sex: On Aggression in Women and Men.* Translated by Craig Tomlinson. New York: Fromm International, 1987.

Moltmann-Wendel, Elisabeth. *A Land Flowing with Milk and Honey: Perspectives on Feminist Theology.* Translated by John Bowden. New York: Crossroad, 1986.

——, ed. *Frau und Religion: Gotteserfahrung im Patriarchat.* Frankfurt: Fischer, 1983.

——, ed. *Frauenbefreiung: Biblische und Theologische Argumente.* 4th ed. Munich: Christian Kaiser, 1986.

Mulack, Christa. *Die weiblichkeit Gottes: Matriarchale Voraussetzungen des Gottesbildes.* Stuttgart: Kreuz, 1983.

Murphy, Yolanda, and Robert Murphy. *Woman of the Forest.* 2nd ed. New York: Columbia University Press, 1985.

Niebuhr, H. Richard. *Radical Monotheism and Western Culture.* New York: Harper, 1960.

Ochshorn, Judith. *The Female Experience and the Nature of the Divine.* Bloomington, In.: Indiana University Press, 1981.

Patai, Raphael. *The Hebrew Goddess.* New York: Ktav Publishing House, 1968.

Paul, Diana Y. *Women in Buddhism: Images of the Feminine in Mahayan Tradition.* 2d ed. Berkeley, Calif.: University of California Press, 1985.

Pereira, Nunes. *Moronguetá: Um Decameron indigena.* 2nd ed. 2 vols. Rio de Janeiro: Civilizacao Brasileira, 1980.

Pickthall, Marmaduke. *The Meaning of the Glorious Koran: An Explanatory Translation.* London: George Allen & Unwin, 1957.

Pritchard, James B., ed. *Ancient Near Eastern Texts Relating to the Old Testament.* 2nd ed. Princeton, N.J.: Princeton University Press, 1955.

Raming, Ida. *The Exclusion of Women from the Priesthood: Divine Law or Sex Discrimination?* Translated by Norman R. Adams. Methuchen, N.J.: Scarecrow Press, 1976.

von Ranke-Graves, Robert. *Die weiße Göttin: Sprache des Mythos.* Reinbek: Rowolt, 1985.

Richter, Horst Eberhard. *All Mighty: A Study of the God Complex in Western Man.* Translated by Jan van Heurck. Claremont, Calif.: Hunter House, 1984.

Römer, Willem H. P. *Frauenbriefe über Religion, Politik, und Privatleben in Mari.* Neukirchen-Vluyn: Neukirchener Verlag, 1971.

Rose, Martin. *Der Ausschließlichkeitsanspruch Jahwes: Deuteronomische Schultheologie und die Volksfrömmigkeit in der späten Königszeit.* Stuttgart: Kohlhammer, 1975.

Ruether, Rosemary Radford. *Sexism and God-Talk: Toward a Feminist Theology.* Boston: Beacon Press, 1983.

Schottroff, Luise. "Maria Magdalena und die Frauen am Grabe Jesu." *Evangelische Theologie* 42 (1982) 3–25.

Schunck, K. D. "bāmāh." In *Theological Dictionary of the Old Testament,* vol. 2, edited by G. Johannes Botterweck and Helmer Ringgren. Translated by John T. Willis, 139–145. Grand Rapids, Mich.: Wm. B. Eerdmans, 1975.

Schüngel-Straumann, Helen. "Gott als Mutter in Hosea 11." *Theologische Quartalschrift* 166 (1986): 119–134.

Schüssler-Fiorenza, Elisabeth. *In Memory of Her: A Feminist Theological Reconstruction of Christian Origins.* New York: Crossroad, 1983.

Seibert, Ilse. *Women in the Ancient Near East.* Translated by Marianne Jerzfeld; revised by George A. Shepperson. New York: Abner Schram, 1974.

Sigrist, Christian. *Regulierte Anarchie: Untersuchungen zum Fehlen und zur Entstehung politischer Herrschaft in segmentaren Gesellschaften in Afrika.* Reprint. Hamburg: Europäische Verlags-Anstalt, 1994.

Smelik, Klaas A. D. *Writings from Ancient Israel: A Handbook of Historical and Religious Documents.* Translated by G. I. Davies. Louisville, Ky.: Westminster John Knox Press, 1991.

Sölle, Dorothee. "Aus der Zeit der Verzweiflung." *JK* 48 (1987): 614–620.

Sorge, Elga. *Religion und Frau: Weibliche Spiritualität im Christentum.* 5th ed. Stuttgart: Kohlhammer, 1988.

Springer, Sally, and Georg Deutsch. *Left Brain, Right Brain.* San Francisco: W. H. Freeman, 1981.

Staden, Hans. *Brasilien: Die wahrhaftige Historie der wilden, nackten, grimmigen Menschenfresser-Leute.* 1550. Reprint, 2nd ed. Tübingen: Thienemann, 1984.

Stamm, Johann Jakob. "Hebräische Frauennamen." In *Beiträge zur hebräischen and altorientalischen Namenkunde.* 97–135. Edited by Ernst Jenni and Martin Klopfenstein. Fribourg: Universitätsverlag; Göttingen: Vandenhoeck & Ruprecht, 1980.

Terrien, Samuel. *Till the Heart Sings: A Biblical Theology of Manhood and Womanhood.* Philadelphia: Fortress Press, 1985.

Tevoedjre, Albert. *Poverty, Wealth of Mankind.* New York: Pergamon Press, 1979.

Thiel, Winfried. *Die soziale Entwicklung Israels in vorstaatlicher Zeit.* 2nd ed. Neukirchen-Vluyn: Neukirchener Verlag, 1985.

Tigay, Jeffrey H. *You Shall Have No Other Gods: Israelite Religion in the Light of Hebrew Inscriptions.* Atlanta: Scholars Press, 1986.

Trible, Phyllis. *God and the Rhetoric of Sexuality.* Philadelphia: Fortress Press.

————. *Texts of Terror: Literary-Feminist Readings of Biblical Narratives.* Philadelphia: Fortress Press, 1984.

Türck, Ulricke. "Die Stellung der Frau in Elephantine als Ergebnis persisch-babylonischen Rechtseinflusses." *Zeitschrift für die Alttestamentliche Wissenschaft* 46 (1928): 166–169.

Turner, Victor W. *The Ritual Process: Structure and Anti-structure.* Chicago: Aldine Publishing, 1969.

Underhill, Ruth. *Red Man's Religion: Beliefs and Practices of the Indians North of Mexico.* 2nd ed. Chicago: University of Chicago Press, 1972.

Vorländer, Hermann. *Mein Gott: Die Vorstellungen vom persönlichen Gott im Alten Orient und im Alten Testament.* Kevelaer: Butzon & Bercker, 1975.

Weiler, Gerda. *Ich verwerfe im Lande die Kriege: Das verborgene Martriarchat im Alten Testament.* Munich: Frauenoffensive, 1984.

Wenck, Inge. *Gott ist im Mann zu kurz gekommen: Eine Frau über Jesus von Nazareth.* Gütersloh: Gütersloher Verlagshaus Gerd Mohn, 1982.

Wesel, Uwe. *Der Mythos vom Matriarchat: Über Bachofens Mutterrecht und die Stellung von Frauen in frühen Gesellschaften vor der Entstehung staatlicher Herrschaft.* Frankfurt: Suhrkamp, 1980.

Winter, Urs. *Frau und Göttin: Exegetische und ikonographische Studien zum weiblichen Gottesbild im Alten Israel und in dessen Umwelt.* Freiburg, Switzerland: Universitätsverlag; Göttingen: Vandenhoeck & Ruprecht, 1983.

Wolkstein, Diane, and Samuel N. Kramer. *Inanna, Queen of Heaven and Earth: Her Stories and Hymns from Sumer.* New York: Harper & Row, 1983.

INDEX OF BIBLICAL REFERENCES

168   INDEX